FROM **BOOK** TO
BESTSELLER

An Insider's Guide to Publicizing and Marketing your Book!

TELEVISION

RADIO

BOOK SIGNINGS

PENNY SANSEVIERI

New York

FROM **BOOK** TO BESTSELLER

An Insider's Guide to Publicizing
and Marketing Your Book!

by Penny C. Sansevieri

© 2007. All rights reserved.

ISBN: 1-60037-084-5 (Hardcover)

ISBN: 1-60037-085-3 (Paperback)

ISBN: 1-60037-086-1 (eBook)

ISBN: 1-60037-087-X (Audio)

Published by:

MORGAN · JAMES
THE ENTREPRENEURIAL PUBLISHER™
www.morganjamespublishing.com

Morgan James Publishing, LLC

1225 Franklin Ave. Ste 325

Garden City, NY 11530-1693

Toll Free 800-485-4943

www.MorganJamesPublishing.com

Habitat
for Humanity®
Peninsula
Building Partner

Interior Design by:
Bonnie Bushman
bbushman@bresnan.net

MORE BOOKS BY
PENNY SANSEVIERI

Nonfiction

Get Published Today
(Morgan James Publishing 2006)

From Book to Bestseller
(PublishingGold.com, Inc. 2005)

No More Rejections: Get Published Today!
(PublishingGold.com, Inc. 2005)

No More Rejections: Get Published Today!
(Infinity Publishing 2002, 2003)

*Get Published! An author's guide to the
online publishing revolution*
(1st Books, 2001)

Fiction

The Cliffhanger
(iUniverse, 2000)

Candlewood Lake
(iUniverse, 2006)

To subscribe to our free newsletter send an e-mail to

subscribe@amarketingexpert.com

We'd love your feedback.
Here's how to contact us:

Author Marketing Experts, Inc.

Post Office Box 421156

San Diego, CA 92142

www.amarketingexpert.com

penny@amarketingexpert.com

For Frans

The best dad a
girl could ever have.

CONTENTS

ACKNOWLEDGMENTS

It would take an entire book to thank everyone involved in the process of creating From Book to Bestseller. Of all the sections in this book, this is no doubt the most difficult to write.

There are scores of people who contribute both in their support and the willingness to share their own creativity. The students in the classes I teach and their tireless efforts to see their work in print; my clients both past and present whom I am enormously fortunate to work with and I am honored that they entrust their work to me.

Many thanks to the "behind the scenes" people who brought their own amazing level of support and creativity to this book for their wisdom and insight and constant and tireless feedback, Paula Krapf, Jeniffer Thompson, Saundra Woolsey, Kathy Gallyer and all the folks at Morgan James Publishing for taking on my family of books and making them their own.

My friends and family who always love and support me even when my schedule doesn't always permit me to spend as much time with them as I'd like.

As a kid I always dreamt of being an author, my fondest wish was to see my work in print. Not only did my dream come true, but the ripple effect of one dream coming true has been many others coming true in the process. I hope in some small way that this book will help you work on a part of your own dream, whatever that might be.

I have many blessings in my life. To list them all here would be endless. I am and always will have a grateful heart for my work and my mission and I am enormously fortunate to be able to do what I love, I wish you the same kind of happiness.

DISCLAIMER

Every attempt has been made to make From Book to Bestseller as accurate and complete as possible. However there may be mistakes both typographical and in content. Therefore the text and information contained in this book should be used only as a general guide. Furthermore, the information contained in this book consists of media contact information, Web site, and promotional tools that are current only up to the printing date.

It is not the purpose of this book to be the single marketing tool in your library and we always recommend the use of other books on book marketing as suggested in our references section.

From Book to Bestseller contains advice on marketing, promotion, and selling books. The use of this book is not a substitute for publishing, business, tax, accounting, consulting or other professional services. Consult the appropriate professionals for answers to your specific questions. Neither the publisher nor the author nor the contributors mentioned in this book bear any liability for the incorrect or improper use of this book or the information and advice contained herein. If you do not wish to be bound by the terms of this paragraph, promptly return this book for a complete refund.

FOREWORD

For a book to be successful, it must be promoted. While this may seem obvious, it's not always a given. Often authors believe the hardest part is behind them once the book is written. It's safe to say, however, that writing the book is the easy part. The work really begins once the book rolls off the presses; for truly savvy authors, the work begins months before the presses even start running. In *From Book to Bestseller*, publicist and media maven Penny Sansevieri has covered virtually every aspect of book promotion and publicity and has provided a gold mine of information, leads, ideas, and sales advice.

There is no one secret to publishing success. Rather, there are many, and Sansevieri has done an excellent job of outlining them in this book in a manner that is easy to understand. Even if you've never done any type of book marketing before, this book will guide you through the process step by step, creatively and effectively. Sansevieri's willingness to share her own knowledge and insider secrets to success, combined with information culled from years of experience, makes *From Book to Bestseller* not only indispensable, but also a literary roadmap to success.

Publishing a book does not guarantee that people will read it; you still have to let them know it's out there. And with 195,000 titles published each year, this is becoming increasingly difficult. Using tools like the book you are holding now will help you on your journey and save you valuable marketing dollars in the process. Use it as a roadmap, a guidebook, and your very own secret to success.

Dan Poynter
ParaPublishing.com

INTRODUCTION

A journey of a thousand miles begins with a single step.
— Chinese proverb

So, do you know when you should start marketing your book? The answer to this question might surprise you. You should start marketing your book before you put pen to paper. Now if you've already finished your tome, don't worry! There are things you can do to insure the success of your book even if the words "book marketing" just entered into your vocabulary.

From Book to Bestseller is geared to any and every stage of book marketing. Whether you are a novice or a pro looking to increase your knowledge, this book will offer guidance, support, and a dash of wisdom to help you launch a successful campaign.

As a book marketing specialist, publicist and author coach, I've worked with writers and authors in varying stages of book creation. Some have yet to give birth to their novel and come to me with only an *idea* of what they want to write, while others have their masterpiece finished and are eager to let the world see what they've written. Most, however, shiver at the thought of marketing their own work. My goal for *From Book to Bestseller* is to take you step-by-step through the process of marketing and assuage any fears you might have had about getting out there and promoting your book. I offer my personal guarantee when I say that by the end of this book you will view book marketing in a new and different light. You'll not only be ready to take this to task but you'll be savvy, skillful and a serious "outside the book" thinker.

Your book can be a success, and you can make it happen!

SECTION ONE

INTRODUCTION TO
BOOK MARKETING

*Excellence is to do a common thing
in an uncommon way.*
—*Booker T. Washington*

BECOMING A
MARKETING GURU

If you don't blow your own horn,
someone else will use it as a spittoon.
— *Anonymous*

The word "book marketing" probably conjures up images of your book filling a bookstore window, or you sitting at a table with eager readers lined up outside the door, all waiting breathlessly for an autographed copy of your book. Well, let me tell you first that book signings are boring and the worst way to sell a book. Why? Because everyone does it. Your marketing campaign should be as unique as your book. That's not to say that you can't do a signing or two, certainly it's every author's right. But book signings alone won't sell your book. In fact, with all the competition out there for that exclusive signing spot, book signings should be at the bottom of the list of things you want to do to promote your book.

If you're still not convinced, consider this: over 195,000 titles are published each year in the United States alone. That figures to approximately 500 titles released each day. Over 1.3 million books are in print or currently available. To display all of these books, a bookstore would need five miles of shelf space. When you consider that most bookstores stock 40,000

3

to 80,000 titles, how in the world are people going to know your book exists? After you do a signing, what will happen to your book? Will it sit on the bookstore shelf amidst the other 80,000 titles? How will people find yours? And to add to this, did you know that only 35% of the American public actually buys their books in a bookstore? So where you might ask, do they get their books? Well, how about gift shops, souvenir shops, specialty stores, Amazon.com, or your Web site just to name a few.

The point here is that while traditional sales channels work, you should look at combining the traditional with the less-than-traditional. Certainly it's great to want to emulate the marketing plans of others but remember, no two books are alike and neither are their audiences or their authors. Better to craft a plan to suit your book than to force your book into a plan that doesn't fit. Get a plan and go for it, one step at a time.

CREATING YOUR UNIQUE MARKETING CAMPAIGN

If the doctor told me I had six minutes to live,
I'd type a little faster.
— Isaac Asimov

There are many different ways to market your book. You can do speaking engagements, get book reviews, do Internet marketing, sell your book to an association as a premium sale item, and many, many, more. *What* you do will depend on a few things. First and foremost, it will depend on the topic of your book and the audience who will read it. Second, it will depend on how much time you have to market your book. Third, it will depend on how much money you have to invest in your writing future. All of these components, put together, will begin to help you define your marketing plan.

Determining Your Goals

Before you launch into your marketing campaign, you should take a hard look at your goals for this book. What you wish to accomplish with it will go a long way to helping you determine what type of marketing campaign you'll need. If your book has major, national appeal, then a bigger, more elaborate campaign might be necessary to get your book into the hands of your readers. Or, let's say you wrote a family memoir that very few people outside your immediate family will want to read. In this case, marketing isn't something you'll need to consider. But, if you want your memoir to be the next *Angela's Ashes*, then you'll need to market it. If your book has a small, focused audience, then a national campaign probably isn't a wise thing to consider. Or, if you've written the book as an extension of your business, then marketing it might consist of writing a few articles for trade journals, and book reviews, maybe even some regular speaking engagements.

Your goals for this book might change as you move through your campaign. Things often outside of your control such as personal life changes and world events can alter your program – sometimes for the better – so keep an eye out for things that can benefit your campaign and take it to a new, and possibly more successful, direction. It's important as you move through your campaign to define and then redefine your goals at appropriate intervals to keep the momentum going, or alternatively, to determine how effective the campaign is that you've been working on.

Different Ways to Market Your Book

There are about as many different marketing methods as there are books. We'll explore most of them in this book, but here are a few of them to start thinking about.

Media Campaign

If your book has media appeal, then you might want to consider getting in front of a producer or reporter and letting them know you have this great story to tell. Be careful with this though. While the lure of the media may seem glamorous and while you might think you have a book Oprah would die to have on her show, there's a lot of competition out there. Often a media campaign on its own doesn't do a whole lot for a book. But, combined with a few other effective strategies, it can help leverage your success greatly.

Speaking Engagements

Getting up in front of a crowded room might seem like a terrifying proposition for you but it's a great way to sell a book. How many books have you bought after you were inspired by one speaker or another? Probably quite a few. Speaking is a great way to spread the message about your topic and your work.

Internet Marketing

These days, Internet marketing is one of the best things you can do for your book. But it's more than just having a Web site, it's about connecting with readers on the Net, it's about virtual networking and it's about digging into the groups that can help you get your book and message directly into the hands of your reader. If your audience surfs the Net (and most readers do), this is a not-to-be overlooked promotional tool. Most authors stop with their Internet promotion once their Web site is up, this is a mistake. It's like I always say: what if you build a Web site and no one shows up. Harnessing the power of the Net means truly "harnessing" it. Don't stop short of the promise of virtual success with a site that no one's heard about, link to other sites and have them link to you, participate in the blogging community, host an online chat, or get your book reviewed online. Internet marketing also includes things like

e-mail campaigns, electronic newsletters (called Ezines) and
even permission marketing.

Special or Premium Sales

This method of promotion involves selling your book in
bulk to companies, organizations, or associations. By "bulk"
I mean sales in the amount of five to 100,000 copies. If your
book ties into a corporate message, association, or other outlet,
you might want to consider this form of promotion. For some
authors, this is the only type of marketing they do and with the
potential for off-the-chart sales, you can imagine why!

SEVEN SECRETS OF WRITING A BOOK THAT SELLS

Giving up was never an option.
— Lance Armstrong

It's one thing to write a book, but it's an entirely different thing to write one that's a saleable, viable, marketable product. Ensuring the success of a book is something even the biggest publishers have never been able to guarantee. Mitigating circumstances, flash trends, and world events will all affect buyer preferences. That said, there are still ways to leverage the sales-factor in your favor and here's how you do it.

1. **Know your readers.** We're not just talking about whether your readers are male or female. You'll want to know a myriad of factors about your audience. How old are your readers (age range)? Are your readers married, single, or divorced? Where do your readers live (generally)? What do your readers do for a living? What other books/publications do they read? Develop a profile that includes where they shop, what clubs they belong to, etc.

These elements will help you incorporate pertinent aspects into your book *and* help you unearth salient marketing opportunities (i.e., publications and stores).

10

2. **Know your market.** What's the market like for your book? Is there a trend out there you're positioning yourself towards? Are you reading all the publications related to this topic/trend? Are there any "holes" out there that your book could fill? What's the future for this market/topic? For example, let's say you're a fiction writer looking to publish chick lit. Go to any bookstore and you can't help but spot the cutsie, pink, cartoonish covers. Many thought this trend was dying out, but it has recently seen another surge. What do you know about trends related to your book/topic/audience?

3. **Read similar books.** What else has been published on your topic? Have you read all 10 books in your category? If you haven't, you should. You'll want to know everything you can about what's out there and how it's being positioned and perceived in the marketplace. It's never a problem having a similar topic. When I published *From Book to Bestseller*, I knew there were other books out there on marketing. I read them all – then angled my book differently.

4. **Get and stay current.** What's going on in your industry today? What are some hot buttons? What are people looking for? What's next on the horizon for this topic/audience? If you can't seem to gather this information through traditional channels, why not survey your target audience? There are a number of places to run free surveys. Survey Monkey (www.surveymonkey.com) is one of them.

5. **Follow the media.** What's the media talking about these days? Keep track of media buzz – what they're paying attention to and what they're writing about. Delve beyond the

front page of your newspaper to the second or third page and see what's filling the pages. If you can get your hands on out-of-state papers, do a comparative review; most newspapers are online these days and can be read for free. Do you see a trend in coverage? Is there something that seems to be getting more buzz even if it's on page six?

6. **Talk. Teach. Listen.** One of the best ways I've found to get in touch with my audience was to teach a class and do speaking engagements. When I was putting together my book, *From Book to Bestseller*, I found that the classes I taught provided valuable information for creating a great book because they put me directly in touch with my audience!

7. **Timing is everything.** When do you plan to release your tome? Are you releasing around a holiday or anniversary? Could you take advantage of any upcoming event and/or holiday for your book launch?

Ethical Bribes

Ethical Bribes So what's an ethical bribe? Well it's something of value that you give your web visitor in order to get something. Like what? Well, for example when you click on my site: Author Marketing Experts and subscribe to this newsletter you a get a list of our Top 50 Media Contacts. No kidding. Names, e-mails, addresses -- the whole shebang.

If you haven't had much luck getting folks to sign up for your newsletter on your site consider offering an "ethical bribe." So what do you get? Well, you get their e-mail address that you can market to via your newsletter. We saw an increase of nearly 50% in signups when we did this and readers love it! They get something of value and we get to stay in touch with the folks who visit our site!

WHO'S YOUR MARKET?

A person who aims at nothing is sure to hit it.
— *Anonymous*

When I talk to authors about their books, one of the first questions I ask them is: Who's your audience? Most authors will smile proudly and say: "Everyone!" Well, guess what folks? If your audience is "everyone" then your market is not focused and you'll have too much competition. By narrowing your market and knowing your reader, you can hone in on a specific group of people. The fact of the matter is that book marketing should begin while the book is still being written. Why? Because your subject matter, your characters, dialogues, etc. will all reflect your specific reader demographic.

For example, if you're writing a novel for the teenage crowd you might want to think about using a setting they can respond to. For most teenagers, it's futuristic. Writing a novel set during the sixties might not entice them to read on. But, if you were writing a book for the baby boomer generation, something set in the sixties might be perfect.

The same holds true for nonfiction. Again, you're writing for a specific market. If it's a how-to book, you'll need to know how advanced your reader is. Are they a beginner or have they had some experience with your topic? The Idiot's Guide books do well because their market is very specific. You might refute this because their subject matter is so broad. But guess what each of their readers has in common? They're all beginners.

When you're beginning your book outline, it probably wouldn't hurt to take a moment to see what everyone else is doing. Get on Amazon.com, BN.com or any one of the online bookstores and see what's out there. Order them or go to your local library. The key here is to find out what's working and what isn't. Know your competition. So what if you're writing something that's already been done. Perhaps you're reinventing the wheel, or, maybe you're looking at the same topic from a different angle. I mean, when I was considering writing this book, I almost gave up when I realized how many books on book marketing there were out there. But, you know what? Mine is different. Yours can be too.

Hey, Big Spender!

Are you marketing to boomer women? If you're not, perhaps you should be, women age 50+ constitute a fairly large market segment. They are the healthiest, wealthiest, most influential generation of women in history, and terms like mature (overripe), middle- aged (frumpy) and senior (out to pasture) fail to convey their vitality and potential.

These women should be the primary marketing target for myriad products including yours! The good news here is that this group is very overlooked by advertisers who have spent a good deal of their time, effort (and yes money) focusing on the youth groups and the "tweens" as they are called. But the

Boomer group of women has time and money to spend and they are probably looking for what you have to sell!

If you've been marketing your book for a while with little or no momentum, think about redefining your reader. I spoke to an associate of mine who is doing this with her book. Initially, her audience seemed obvious. But, as she began marketing she realized it was in fact an entirely different age group. Sometimes that happens. You'll be marketing your book to one particular group when you realize they're not your target at all. Sometimes this can't be avoided, sometimes book marketing isn't the exact science we'd like it to be. Still, asking yourself a few specific questions can probably help save you valuable marketing dollars and even more valuable time.

Here are some questions to help you better define your audience:

- How old is my reader?
- Is my reader male or female?
- Where does my reader live?
- How educated is my reader?
- What makes my reader happy?
- What saddens my reader?
- What are their fears?
- What are their aspirations?
- What do they need most in their life?
- What does my reader do for a living?

- Is my reader married, single, or divorced?

- Is my reader a parent?

- What does my reader do in his or her spare time?

- What magazines or publications do they read?

- What types of books does my reader already enjoy?

By knowing some or all of the above, you'll really be able to get a handle on who you're marketing to. As you dig into the life of your reader all sorts of things will begin to emerge. For example, possible associations they belong to and magazines and books they read. This will not only tell you how to market effectively, but also allow you to create a book that feels as though it was written just for your reader. A book that when finished, will excite and enlighten them and make them want to pass it on. Think about this for a second. How many times have you finished a book and said: "Well, the first part was good, but the last three chapters were kind of a waste of my time." Making your reader feel good, informed or entertained from start to finish will not only leave you with a happy reader, but a walking, talking advertisement for your book and a fan for all of your future works.

When you know who your market is, you can begin a more directed campaign. Also, you can begin to join some online newsgroups related to your market, organizations or other areas that can draw attention to your book. Also, by joining groups related to your book, you will begin to learn about other areas for potential sales. For example, if your book is senior citizen related, you can begin to explore magazines, newsletters and communities directed at seniors. If your book is related to children of divorced parents, you have a whole different area to pursue. Try hooking up with local organizations such as PWP (Parents without Partners). Offer to do a talk at one of their meetings. When you join online newsgroups; offer advice; be helpful. Try to find any and all trade magazines related to your topic. If you are writing a book about gardening, I know for a fact that there are at least 50 gardening magazines and newsletters in my area alone to get you started. If your book is a mystery, try joining some mystery groups and online chats. Check out www.about.com and head to their reading room section. You'll find a myriad of selections from which you can choose.

Marketing Tip:

Did you know that women over 40 are soon to be the largest and the wealthiest demographic in the country? If you're not currently targeting this group of women, you might want to consider doing so.

NEVER (EVER)
SELL YOUR BOOK

*The beautiful part of writing is that you don't have to get
it right the first time, unlike, say, a brain surgeon.*
— *Robert Cromier*

So you're all ready to promote your book. You've got
a great press kit, a polished bio, and a letter-perfect press
release. Now you're ready to sell, sell, sell, right? Wrong.
One of the biggest mistakes authors make is selling their
books. Remember it's not about the book, it's about what the
book can do for the reader.

Finding the benefits to your book might seem like a pretty
simple task and touting that "It's a great read!" won't get you
very far. To determine what your book will do for your reader,
you'll have to dig deep, sometimes deeper than you thought.
Especially if your book is fiction, this task of finding benefits
will require some serious brainstorming. The key here is, be
different. If you have a diet book, don't offer the same benefits
a million other books do: you'll lose weight. Instead, offer a
benefit that is decidedly different than anything that's out there.
Or, try to couch a similar benefit in a different way. At the end
of the day, it's all about the WIIFM factor: what's in it for me.

If your reader likes what's in it for them, they'll buy your book - otherwise they'll just move on.

The idea of not selling your book also holds true when you're doing an interview. Never, ever answer an interviewer's question with: "You'll find it in my book." Because the fact is you're an author, of course the answer is in your book, but right now you're there to help them with their interview, save the sales pitches for another time.

The uniqueness of your benefits can also directly relate to the particular audience you're speaking to. For example if you have different levels of readers or readers from different backgrounds, it's a good idea to work up a set of benefits for each of them, that way any interview you do (or speaking engagement) will offer benefits with the audience in mind as opposed to a more generic form of "Here's what my book can do for you!" Creating a list of benefits for your book can aid your campaign in a number of ways, first it'll help you get away from a more "salesy" type of approach and second, it will help you create the tip sheets that can help add substance to your press kit. If you're working on the benefit angle of your book early enough, you can incorporate these into the back copy of your book.

The point is, never, ever sell your book, be a step ahead of the competition and sell what your book can do for the reader and let them know why it's better than the competition. In the end, that's all anyone will care about.

Trend Spotting Anyone?

If you're interested to see what's hot and what's not on the web, click on over to the following sites. They're packed with info on searches and hot new trends!

http://buzz.yahoo.com/
http://www.trendwatching.com/
http://www.pollingreport.com/

SMART BUDGETING

Money is better than poverty, if only for financial reasons.
— Woody Allen

So, what's all this going to cost you? When I interviewed Eric Gelb, MBA and Editor of PublishingGold.com, Inc. (www. publishinggold.com), he tallied up a list for our readers and offered the following advice: "Be cautious about where you put your money when you're promoting your book. It can take a while to see results and you want to make sure you're able to be in this for the long-haul." He suggested setting realistic expectations for yourself. "And," he advised, "don't even think about renting office space unless you have another business that can sustain it."

Here are a few items he suggested you consider as you're promoting your book and getting into the business of publishing.

One-time expenses
- Filing fees for incorporation
- Filing fees for copyright
- Copy Editor
- Domain name purchase

- Web designer
- Additional phone line
- Equipment (printer/computer)
- Stationery
- Bookmarks
- Postcards
- Business cards
- Computer programs (software)
- Headshot
- Galley/review copies of your book
- Business license

On-going expenses

- Web hosting
- Answering service/voice mail system
- Additional phone line
- Mobile phone
- Telephone calls
- Faxing fees
- Book publicist/Media relations specialist
- Finished copies of your book
- Post Office Box
- Postage

- Mailers

- Magazine subscriptions

- Professional dues and memberships

- Photocopies

- Merchant account fees (for credit card sales)

- Intellectual property attorney

- Accountant

- Bank account

- Travel fees associated with book promotion

- Insurance if you maintain any sizable inventory

"Keep in mind," says Gelb, "that many of these items are likely to be tax deductible since the expenditures relate to your business; be sure to hook up with a qualified accountant or other tax advisor to be certain what you can and can't deduct. Smart planning will help you manage your money and keep more of what you earn."

WINNING THE NAME GAME

*I take the view, and always have, that if you cannot
say what you are going to say in twenty minutes
you ought to go away and write a book about it.*

— *Lord Brabazon*

How many of you have spent hours or days toiling over the title for your book? My first book, *The Cliffhanger*, was renamed probably six times before I stayed with the current title. Naming your book can be difficult, especially if the book will work as a sort of branding for everything else you do. Nonfiction books are often seen as a stepping stone to speaking engagements, product launches, and a variety of other business endeavors. In fact, the naming of a nonfiction or business book is so critical that a poorly chosen title can actually make or break a book's success. If you're in the midst of picking a name, or planning future titles, there are some basic strategies you should consider before you finalize your book cover:

The name of your book *must* tell people what it's about. If you try to be clever and make them guess, your potential customer will just put it down and move on to a title they do understand.

Put the benefit right in the name - for example *Chicken Soup for the Soul* tells you right up front that, much like a cup of chicken soup when you're sick, this book is going to make you feel better. If this leaves you feeling perplexed, take a moment to list five benefits of your book. Once you have those benefits listed, slowly but surely a book title will begin to emerge.

Think about all the different uses you might be able to derive from the name of your book. Is it going to be on your Web site? Is it a stand alone book or part of a product line? Is this book one of a series? Determining the exact uses of this title will help you define it further.

And finally, go see what the competition is doing. Spend an afternoon at the bookstore and see what titles have worked well for similar books in your genre.

Other Naming Tips

Did you know that some words are easier to remember than others? Sound odd? Not really. Language experts will tell us that we just react differently to certain sounds. The letters K and P for example are what language experts call "plosives." A plosive is a little bit of language that pops out of your mouth and draws attention to itself. A plosive is a "stopper" in language. A plosive makes us pause for emphasis when we say it. The letters B, C, D, K, P and T are all plosives.

What's especially interesting is that brand names beginning with plosives have higher recall scores than non-plosive names. Several studies of the top 200 brand names have made that point. Examples: Bic, Coca-Cola, Kellogg's, Kodak, Pontiac, etc. If you've picked a title for your book or a name for your business or product line that is "unusual" - you might want to check the meaning first. That goes for foreign translation as well. A word or phrase in one language may be fine, but could have a derogatory or opposite meaning once it's translated. Here are a few examples of names that were chosen without the proper research:

- In 1997 Reebok issued a mass recall of their new women's running shoe dubbed "Incubus" - a savvy news reporter brought to their attention the fact that incubus means: "*an evil spirit believed to descend upon and have sex with women while they sleep.*"

- Estée Lauder stopped short of exporting their line of Country Mist makeup to Germany when managers pointed out that "mist" in Germany is slang for manure.

- Trying to be clever, the folks at Guess Jeans placed the Japanese characters "ge" and "su" next to a model in Asian magazines, intending them to mean "Guess." But "gesu" translated in Japanese means "vulgar," "low class" or "mean spirited."

Stumped for a name? Try heading over to The Naming Newsletter (www.namingnewsletter.com). While this site is designed primarily for naming and/or branding companies, there's a lot of great information on titling strategies and tips that can translate easily to your book title.

WRITER'S CONFERENCES

*Writing is easy: All you do is sit staring at a blank sheet of
paper until drops of blood form on your forehead.*
— *Gene Fowler*

Writer's conferences come in all shapes and sizes. Virtually
anytime of the year you can attend a conference anywhere
around the country. But, why would you? Just when your
manuscript is gaining momentum or nearing completion, why
on earth would you put it down to go hang out with a bunch
of writers you've never met? Because despite the notion that
writing is all about isolating yourself, isolation is not a good
thing. No one can live in a vacuum these days. And while it's
great to immerse yourself in reading everything you can on
book promotion and publicity, it's a good idea to connect with
others who are also out there promoting their books.

If you're so tired of hearing about the shrinking publishing
or media market you want to scream, then you really need to
leave the comfort of your office and hustle yourself down to
a conference. There, you will begin to experience every facet
of book promotion. You'll even get the opportunity to make
an appointment or get "face time" with agents, publishers,
publicists, and even a producer or two. But before you send in

your registration form, there are a few things you should know about conferences.

First, keep in mind that not all conferences are created equal. Some are more advanced than others. Some conferences are for published authors, offering them unlimited promotional advice and classes, while other conferences focus only on the craft of writing. If you're at the stage of promoting your book, you'll probably want to stay away from writing classes and instead, focus on meeting people who can make a difference to your campaign.

When selecting a conference, don't get caught up in the glitz of meeting your favorite author if none of the other speakers seem to suit your project. Face it, if the author you so adore goes on tour, chances are pretty likely he or she will be stopping by your city to do a signing anyway. But producers, publicists, and publishers are a different story. Unless you make it a habit of "doing lunch" in New York City on a regular basis, the likelihood of a producer coming within pitching distance outside of a writer's conference is minimal.

So, let's say you've decided on a conference and have your eyes set on several producers, publicists or publishers you want to make appointments with. Before you schedule times with any of these folks, you'll want know a little bit about them. For example, nothing will end a meeting faster than sitting down with someone who doesn't handle your angle or story. Doing your research can really benefit you. If you're meeting with a producer, take a minute to peruse their Web site for past stories they've worked and take a minute to learn a bit about them. Depending on their background and interests, you might be able to weave some of this into your pitch to them during your face to face meeting. If your target is a publicist, their Web sites usually indicate the type of projects they manage.

Once you have your appointment, be ready to pitch all of your angles. Remember to have your "elevator pitch" ready. You'll want to keep your pitches quick, succinct and interesting! If the agent, producer or publicist doesn't look interested, move onto the next item and try to learn from the rejections you do get.

One of the things people don't often consider at these events is the networking factor. Done correctly, networking can bring about amazing results. You never know who knows someone who knows someone who can help you further your marketing goals. Or perhaps you're looking for an editor or illustrator. I can almost guarantee you'll find what you need by networking. Writer's conferences are not a place to be shy. Walk up to people and start a conversation with them and don't be afraid to speak to a presenter if you catch them between talks. As a frequent presenter at conferences I can tell you, this is why we are there - to help you, the author. Our sole purpose for attending these events is to share what we know.

If you are attending a conference that lasts longer than a day, you'll quickly start making friends with other writers and want to "hang out" with them. This is great for building relationships but terrible for networking. Mingle and talk with as many other attendees or presenters as you can. During lunch, make sure you sit at a table with people you don't know. Introduce yourself, ask your fellow conference attendees about their projects and then start talking about yours. Ask lots of questions, take your business cards (or bookmarks) and always keep a pad and pen handy.

With the right planning, a writer's conference can be
enormously successful and while they may not always lead to
immediate marketing or publicity results, they are certainly a
step in the right direction!

Here are a few writer's conferences you might want to
think about attending:

PMA Publishing University
    http://www.pma-online.org

Whidbey Island Writer's Conference
    www.writeonwhidbey.org/Conference/

Maryland Writer's Conference
    www.marylandwriters.org

Small Press Association (SPAN)
    www.spannet.org

Willamette Writer's Conference
    www.willamettewriters.com

Romance Writers of America
    www.rwanational.org

San Francisco Writer's Conference
    www.sfwriters.org

Printer's Row Book Fair
    http://www.chicagotribune.com/extras/printersrow/
    index.html

Maryland Writers Association Annual Writer's Conference
www.marylandwriters.org

Washington Writer's Conference
www.washwriter.org

Los Angeles Times Festival of Books
www.latimes.com/festivalofbooks

Get Published Today! Workshops
Offered throughout the country from Author Marketing
Experts, Inc.

For more information, or to find out when they're coming to
your area, send an e-mail to classes@amarketingexpert.com

Writer's Conference Ice Breakers

Cat got your tongue when it comes to breaking the ice
at a writer's conference? Here are a few quick ways to get
a conversation going with a speaker or fellow conference
participant. Remember that while you're there to further your
career, you'll keep a conversation going a lot longer if you
inquire about the things that interest other people. You never
know where the conversation will go from there!

*   What are some publishing trends a new writer needs to
    be aware of?

*   What's your favorite project right now?

- What's the best thing a writer can do for his or her career?

- How did you get into the publishing business?

The Return of the Writer's Conference

Would you want to go back to the same writer's conference over and over again? You bet. Why? Well when you find a conference you're comfortable with (and one that frequently rotates speakers) you don't have the "learning curve" you do with new events and can dig in and start learning that much sooner. This doesn't mean that you're getting the same information over and over again. Often conferences will offer "tracks" or congruent sessions. You can vary the tracks or sessions you attend each time you return, every year becoming more and more advanced.

YOUR PUBLICATION DATE

The road to success is always under construction.
— Unknown

When you first begin to market your book you'll start to hear the term "publication date" quite a bit. In basic terms, the date your book is available. At the same time, it doesn't have to be the exact date that your book rolls off the presses, in fact your book will probably be "done" long before you hit your publication date. If this sounds confusing, you're not alone.

Publication dates (also referred to as pub dates) were developed a long time ago, back when publishers planned large, elaborate nationwide publicity campaigns. A book's publication date was generally the day the author started their book tour. Since most of the elaborate campaigns have fallen by the wayside, publication dates aren't as crucial as they once were. Still, most book reviewers live and die by publication dates. They do this so they can plan their reviews in a more timely fashion. As you begin to pursue book reviews you'll find that some reviewers need books "three to four months prior to the pub date" or only review books that are past their publication date. Selecting a publication date that gives you a sufficient window to access these reviewers will be crucial to the success of your book.

Reviewers receive on average of 2,500 to 3,500 titles per month. And while they won't review everything they receive, more often than not, you must allow ample review time to be considered (I discuss these terms at length in the "Let's Review" section of this book). According to Jim Cox of the Midwest Book Review, they receive an average of 1,500 titles per month. "So in addition to the physical appearance of their book, the content of their book, the quality of their publicity release and/or media kit, the very timing of submissions, has a great deal to do with how the small press can successfully compete with the large publishers for a reviewer's attention."

If you're not self-published then your publisher will probably pick the date for you, if you are publishing yourself you will have considerably more leeway in selecting this. When you do, I suggest that you tie your publication date into a specific event or anniversary that might be significant to the book. Generally, publishers bring out books in the fall and in the spring. But the savvy marketing individual realizes that there are in fact, many more dates to choose from. Think of Mother's Day, Valentine's Day, Father's Day, Secretary's Day, Easter, Passover, Fourth of July, Halloween, Thanksgiving and of course, Christmas.

When deciding on your publication date, do some research on the Internet or dig out your calendar to determine appropriate dates or possible tie-ins with your book. You can also get a copy of Celebrate Today (www.celebratetoday.com) to find any and all holidays, anniversaries, or possible upcoming events you could hang your star on. If your book ties into a woman-related topic, you can log onto www.womenscalendar.org to find an appropriate tie-in.

KNOW YOUR CATEGORY

Author: A fool, who, not content with having
bored those who have lived with him,
insists on tormenting the generations to come.
— Montesquieu

Knowing what category your book is in will go a long way to helping you to further determine your audience. The Book Industry Systems Advisory Committee (BISAC) has developed over 2,000 subjects and subject codes used to describe the contents of a specific title. From those 2,000 different subject categories, 46 major categories have emerged. Knowing what these are will help you determine where your book fits into the grand scheme of things and how bookstores will shelve your book, should they decide to carry it.

- Antiques/Collectibles

- Architecture

- Biography/Autobiography/Letters

- Business/Economics/Finance

- Computer Technology & Software

- Cookbooks/Cookery

- Crafts/Hobbies

- Current Affairs
- Drama
- Education/Teaching
- Family/Child Care/Relationships
- Fiction/Literature
- Foreign Language Instruction & Reference
- Games
- Gardening/Horticulture
- Health/Fitness
- History
- Home Improvement/Construction
- Humor
- Language Arts
- Law
- Literary Criticism/Essays
- Mathematics
- Medical/Nursing/Home Care
- Music
- Nature/Natural History
- Occultism/Parapsychology
- Performing Arts
- Pets/Pet Care
- Philosophy/Photography
- Poetry
- Political Science/Government

- Psychology/Psychiatry
- Reference
- Religion/Bibles
- Science
- Self-Actualization/Self-Help
- Social Sciences
- Sports/Recreation
- Study Aids
- Technology/Industrial Arts
- Transportation
- Travel/Travel Guides
- True Crime

If your title does not fit into any of these categories, contact:

R.R. Bowker Data Collection Center
P.O. Box 6000-0103
Oldsmar FL 34677-0103
(800) 521-8110 (Reed Reference)
E-mail: info@reedref.com

You can also contact:

Books in Print
www.booksinprint.com
(908) 464-6800
(908) 219-0272

They might be able to guide you to your correct category choice.

SECTION TWO

CREATING AN EXCEPTIONAL PRESS KIT

*Time has convinced me of one thing: Television
is for appearing on — not for looking at.*
— Noel Coward

BECOMING AN EXPERT

If the world should blow itself up, the last audible
voice would be that of an expert saying it can't be done.
— *Peter Ustinov*

The funny thing about writing a book is that the minute you do, you're considered an expert on that particular topic. And, if you did the appropriate research for it, you probably already are – even without realizing it! The key to many a successful campaign is positioning yourself as an expert. The media, for one, loves experts. You only have to turn on CNN during some sort of crisis to find that out. If you're a fiction author you are probably shaking your head right now saying, "how can I be an expert on mystery?" You can, and here's how: find the reality-based topic behind the story. Ever heard of a writer named Tom Clancy? He writes military fiction, right? Well, he's called upon to be a military expert since he's done so much research and he (or his savvy PR person) has positioned him as an expert in that category.

The trick here is to find the story behind the story; the one thing you can hang your star on. So, let's say that your book is about a woman who has overcome domestic abuse. Well, I bet you've done a lot of research about domestic violence and you are probably somewhat of an authority on the subject. I was once working with a mystery author, Austin Camacho, and for his positioning I recommended that he become the authority on the country's most well-known and lesser well-known unsolved mysteries. That, then, became his area of expertise. That would get him in the media. Then, whenever another story hit the media about an unsolved mystery, Austin could step in and comment. The same is true for a WWII Veteran I work with. When the second war in Iraq broke out, I positioned him as an expert. Certainly he could not comment on the new war, but he could talk about what it was like for him when he fought in the Second World War. And while his book was a fictional story surrounding WWII, it was obviously based on fact and factual situations.

Let's say for example that you've written a story that has a basis in reality but might not be so compelling that the media will clamor for your expertise. A good example of this is when my first book, The Cliffhanger, was published. While the story was great, it was about people in love and in denial. What's news about that? So, instead I decided to position myself differently. I decided to make my story about the fact that I was one of the first authors in San Diego to publish via a print-on-demand publisher. That, then, became my story. That's what I hung my star on. Sometimes the connection will be a little tougher to find, but it's there nonetheless, all you have to do is look.

Now, if you're a nonfiction author this becomes a much simpler process. But in either case I recommend that you position yourself as an expert whenever possible. This will not only open media doors for you, but other avenues of promotion as well. You can, for example, obtain speaking assignments at related events and conferences. When you do a book signing you can do a talk as well, positioning yourself again as an authority on a particular subject.

Once you've established yourself as an expert, you're going to want to tap into those markets. Much like what we discussed in the chapter "Who's Your Market," you want to dial into your focused area and become aware of events you can participate in or changes to the market you can comment on. All of this will not only help you leverage media, but keep you on the cutting edge of your topic as well. Then, once you've done this you can offer yourself up on a silver platter to virtually any media outlet with your book and expertise. Later in this book we'll discuss exactly how to do that. For now though, find your pool of fish and navigate the waters.

MEDIA KITS

I once asked this literary agent what writing
paid the best, and he said, "ransom notes."
— Get Shorty

A lot has been said about these handy things, but one idea reigns supreme. They must be creative and they must look professional. Don't waste an editor or producer's time by sending out a media kit packed full of stuff no one will be interested in.

There are a few important things every media kit should include:

- Cover Letter

- Author Bio

- Fact sheet with the following information on it: Book Title, Author, Publisher, ISBN, Price, Pub Date, Type of Book i.e. Hard Cover or Trade Paper

- News Release

- Tip Sheet

- Interview Questions

- Newspaper Clippings (Review clippings)

- Newsletter

We'll go into all the various components in a minute but let me first focus on the final item mentioned on this list, the newsletter. It's something I created several years ago to include in my media kit and I've gotten rave reviews on it.

A newsletter is a simple, preferably colorful, way to highlight all the activity surrounding your book's release. This serves two purposes. First, it alleviates a busy reporter having to sift through your entire media kit, which they probably won't do unless your name is Dean Koontz, and it also spotlights activity in a one page, (or double sided if it's two pages) colorful, easy-to-read newsletter. And, by all means, go to two pages if it becomes too crowded. You don't want to make it tough to read. You want it to be easy to scan. I usually include a column on author appearances, a list where the book is available and any places where it's gotten reviewed. If the review is bad, just say: "Reviewed by XXX" (replace the XXX with the publication name or reviewer). You'll also want to list any awards you've gotten for it, or anything else of merit. Remember to highlight here, not elaborate. That's what all the rest of the information in your media kit is for!

KISS

People's attention span is shorter today than ever. Remember this factoid as you draft your marketing materials. Keep paragraphs short, and statements quick and punchy. Ideally, paragraphs should be six to seven lines in length. Anything longer will seem a lot less inviting to your reader.

INTERVIEW QUESTIONS

One who asks a question is a fool for five minutes;
one who does not ask a question remains a fool forever.
— Chinese Proverb

When putting together a media kit, the savvy PR person knows they should include a list of 10 or so questions for the interviewer to ask them. Some of the best interview questions are the ones that really delve into the topic of the book. Keep in mind that while the reporter or interviewer will want to put you in the best light, they also want an interesting interview. By "interesting" I mean that perhaps it might be slightly hard-hitting or controversial. When you're putting together your list of questions, make sure and include the tough ones too. Think Tom Brokaw. If you don't include them, I can almost guarantee you that a reporter somewhere along the line will ask them anyway.

You might find as you set out to create your own list of questions that this is a considerable challenge, largely due to the fact that you're so close to your own work. It might help you to think back to other events or interviews you've done in the past. See if you can recall some of the questions that were asked then and make sure and include those on your question sheet. If you haven't done events and are stumped, start asking friends or people who have purchased your book. Have a brainstorming session if you can. Come up with 20 questions and then whittle them down to 10 or 12. You can often mix and match these questions depending on the interviewer and slant you are taking with the interview.

Once you've gotten your list of questions down, ask someone to role-play with you. Get a friend or colleague (someone who can be objective) to run through the questions for you. Any problems, issues, or holes in your questions (maybe you forgot to include something very important) will become evident during this role-play and you can make changes before they are included in your press kit. This will also give you an idea of flow and direction, whether the questions make sense. Are they interesting enough? Do they delve into the topic enough? How do the answers "feel?" Remember that the media is all about feelings. Whether it's happy, sad, or enraged, make sure your questions tap into whatever emotions are appropriate to your topic.

Here are a few ideas to get you started on creating your own list of questions for your media kit:

- What's the single thing you want the listener/viewer to know about your book?

- What problem does your book solve?

- Why did you write this book?

- If your book addresses a specific issue or issues, what's the most important thing the viewer/listener needs to know about this?

- Are there new developments related to this topic and if so, what are they?

- What three things can someone do right now to help them with whatever your topic is? Or, if it's fiction, what three things does your book give the reader? An escape? A thrill ride?

TIP SHEET

When something can be read without effort,
great effort has gone into its writing.
— Enrique Jardiel Poncela

Tip sheets are fun and the media loves them! They will often excerpt them for reprinting purposes or use them as sidebars in an article they are writing about you or the topic. Tip sheets are an easy, simple and fun way to break down your book into various elements. Ideally, tip sheets should be five to seven or 10 things exclusive to your book. For example, if you have a dieting book, list 10 ways to lose weight. A beauty book? Ten tips to be more beautiful today. The tips should also have a short explanation by them. But you can also create a tip sheet with tips alone, in other words just a one-line eye catching sentence. If you're stumped for ideas, go hang out in your grocery story and scan the covers of magazines. Magazine covers are great examples of tip sheets, in my opinion. In a few sentences they've just described all the benefits you're going to get by purchasing their magazine. This is the general idea behind creating an effective tip sheet. For example, a tip sheet on the topic of getting on radio and TV tomorrow might be:

- Never pitch your topic on a Monday - that's the busiest day of the week!

- Try to give your topic a local spin on a national story.

- If you're pitching TV, pitch early in the day. Try to get the producer before they go into their daily planning meeting in case they're in need of a story for that day!

- Try pitching any fun or fluff pieces on a Thursday - the slowest news day of the week!

Once you've gotten your tip sheet together, you'll want to include a header and footer on it. If you're not sure how to do this, ask someone who can help you. It will be very important to include at the top of your tip sheet the following sentence: *"Permission to use or excerpt with proper attribution."* This will allow the media to pull from this list and excerpt it as needed, without someone calling to get your permission because you've already given it to them in writing. If the media person is on a time crunch (as most are) they can pull from your tips to complete their article and voila! Media for you, and a finished story for them!

AUTHOR BIO;
IT'S ALL ABOUT YOU

Be yourself. Everyone else is already taken.
—Unknown

So, what's the secret to a great author bio? Just enough information without overwhelming them. As you're creating your bio, keep in mind that the information on it needs to be relevant to the book. This means that you want to list any achievements, schooling, or research you've done related to your work. When a media professional looks at this bio, the first thing they're going to want to know is what gives you the right to write this book? It's all about the credential factor. But don't let this deter you from crafting an exceptional bio. If you think that all the media cares about is educational background, think again. If your topic requires a degree of some sort, then make sure and list that. But, if your book is on, let's say, Elvis memorabilia, then I doubt any kinds of college courses are going to impress a media person (Elvis 101 anyone?). Instead, keep in mind that if you've written about your passion, let's say in this case it's Elvis, you probably have every bit of memorabilia imaginable and you probably know more about this topic (or should) than anyone else out there. That's what makes you the expert in the media's eyes. Conversely, if you've written a romance novel, you might not want to talk about past loves but instead mention any kind of contests you've won, events you've participated in and/or classes you took on the craft of writing.

I've had many people ask me, "Can a bio be funny?" Yes, absolutely, especially if you've written a funny book. Funny where appropriate, serious when warranted. And include a picture of yourself. A picture tends to personalize your bio a bit more and, if you're not including headshots with your kit, the media will want to know what you look like.

To get you started on your bio, make a list of 10 to 15 things the media needs to know about you and then start putting them together. Remember to keep it brief, ideally no more than 300 words should suffice and always, always list your Web site! A template I've used before follows this chapter but keep in mind that as long as it looks professional, any format should do.

Bio Template:

Author Name, *list any degrees here*

Novelist • Author • Entrepreneur

These items should describe in 2-3 bullets about you and your work

Author bio - background

Two to three paragraphs

Author currently resides in Anytown, State.

You can visit his or her Web site at www.Website.com

PRESS RELEASE SAVVY

Charlie Brown, reading a letter to Snoopy: "It's from
your publisher. They printed one copy of your novel.
It says they haven't been able to sell it. They say
they're sorry, your book is now out of print."
— The Literary Ace Strikes Again

It's often said that press releases should only be used for major events. I disagree with this statement. Take a look at some major companies. Go into their investor relations section or company information. There you will usually find a lot of press releases on anything and everything the company has to announce. They can cover job promotions, improved products or even personnel changes. When planning your marketing strategy, I say, "less is less." Go for the big time. If you can get your name in front of someone at least seven times over the next 18 months then you've, at the very least, caught their attention. That's what it takes, according to leaders in the marketing and promotions industry. So think about what you want to announce. First and foremost, will be this wonderful book you just wrote. Then, every time some event occurs surrounding this release, write something about it. Tell the world! Of course, don't overdo it, or people will become wise to you and think you're always crying wolf. But when an event merits mentioning, by all means, mention it. Got a book signing? Send a press release. Did you sell your 10,000th book? By all means, send a press release.

Think about it this way; conversations evaporate. Begin seeing your book as a conversation. You have to manage it, keep it going, and keep people talking. That's your objective (that, and selling a million books, but we'll get to that later). It is up to you to educate the media on you and your book. This gives you name recognition, visibility and credibility. Manage this conversation, and manage it right. You'll find people will start talking about your book. Now, if you think that sending one press release will generate enough conversation to get people interested, think again. Unless you have some major, unbelievable hook, it will probably take hundreds of releases to create that clamored-after "buzz" we always hear everyone talk about. But keep it up. A hundred releases really aren't that many, and you'll be amazed how quickly you blow through your ream of paper when announcement time comes around.

Press release template:

FOR IMMEDIATE RELEASE

CONTACT:

Contact person

Company Name (Optional)

Telephonenumber

Fax number

E-mail address

Web site address

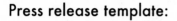

Photo of
your book
cover

Headline

(You *really* need draw their attention with this one.
This is no time for a ho-hum headline!)

Title of your book in BIG BOLD LETTERS

PLACE, DATE – **Opening paragraph:** This paragraph should contain the most important elements: who, what, when, where and why. Make them want to continue reading. The first line of this release is called the "date line" (San Diego, California, November 2, 2005). You do not need to include the date with this. In fact, if your release is going to be used over and over again I recommend omitting the date. If, however, you are releasing something for a specific event (Veteran's Day, Mother's Day) then put the date in there so the media knows it's timely and up-to-date!

Body: This area should include information relevant to your book. Don't ramble on here. Keep it brief. Stress the positive or the angle.

Closing paragraph: This paragraph should include a short summation of your book info, a short author bio or company history, and how they can obtain their free review copy.

The following information should be at the very bottom of your press release:

Title of your book	Author:
Format	ISBN:
Publication Date:	XXX Pages (number of pages)
Price:	Size: (book size)
Available from: Your publisher	To order call: publisher's
	order number

At the very bottom of your release should be the words (centered) - - 30 - - or ###. This tells the media that the release is complete and that there are no more pages.

###

What if your press release goes longer than one page? Ideally, it's best to keep your press release to one page, but if you MUST go to a second page this is how to do a page break:

-more-

(top of second page)

Headline – abbreviated (page 2)

Remainder of text.

Then close with the end comment as discussed above and specific book information below that. Do not repeat this book information on both pages as it becomes confusing, and too much of it will detract from your release.

Did you know?

Pretend for a moment that you're a busy editor. Phones are ringing off the hook, stories are breaking and someone has just handed you a press release. You've only got time to read the first three lines of this release before you decide whether to keep it or have it hit the circular file.

Make those first three lines count!

Components of a Successful Press Release:

- It must be newsworthy.

- Remember, even though I've outlined some specific guidelines for you, press releases aren't a one-size fits all kind of a thing. Tailor them to your media, your book and your target audience.

- Know your audience. Who will be reading your press release?

- Make it simple. Keep it short and write your release in such a way that a busy reporter could easily reuse it for their story.

- Remember the first three-line rule. Your first 10 words must be effective.

- Don't misquote; deal with facts and make sure they are accurate.

- Make sure your press release has substance to it and don't pitch needlessly. Eventually the media will be on to you and you'll get ignored.

- Do you have some pithy quotes or reviews you can add? Then by all means include them. Reporters love quotes.

- Provide all of your contact information: address, phone, fax, e-mail, and Web site.

- Make sure your press release is in the proper format.

- If you're sending your press release via e-mail, copy and paste it into the body of the text. Don't send it as an attachment, unless they've specifically asked you to do this. It WILL get deleted.

- If you can send a press release with a customized cover letter, all the better. Offer a story suggestion in your letter, or play on a story they've recently featured and suggest a follow-up.

Here are some great places to post your press release for free:

- www.click2newsites.com/press.asp

- www.ebookbroadcast.com

- www.pressbox.co.uk

- www.prWeb.com

- www.free-press-release.com/submit/free-press-release. php

- www.i-newswire.com/submit_free.php

- www.press-base.com/add-press.html

- www.clickpress.com/releases/index.shtml

- www.prleap.com/

- www.pressmethod.com/

- http://www.free-press-release.com/

- http://prfree.com/

- http://www.24-7pressrelease.com

Once your press release is done, post it to one of these sites and watch your exposure soar.

Ready, Set, Launch!

Trying to decide when to send out your release? If it's business related, avoid contacting the press between the 15th and 22nd of April, July, and October. That's when publicly held companies release quarterly earnings reports. As for days of the week, Monday is the worst day to send your release. The best day? Thursday. Thursdays are notoriously slow news days.

Stuff the Media Hates

Save your money and your reputation. If you're sending a news release, don't overnight your release or send it as a single item in an envelope with no media kit or cover letter. And speaking of media kits... don't overstuff them. Save the overstuffing for your Thanksgiving turkey and keep the media kits crisp, relevant and easy to navigate!

One final note on media kits: several books on this topic will encourage you to use black for your media kits. I say: "Why?" It's depressing and it's what everyone else is doing. When I send my media kit and review copy to media outlets they have told me that one of the reasons they were more inclined to look at my package (rather than the 40 other ones they received that day) was because mine was the only one that wasn't black. It stood out. Your media kit should do the same.

EXPERT SHEETS

The expert at anything was once a beginner.
—Hayes

One day, I was on a conference call with a morning show producer who said that she wished she had a list of available experts in every imaginable category. That way, when she needed an expert, she could very easily find one. I realized that most producers probably shared her sentiment. That led me to wonder how I could make sure to keep my "expert" clients in the forefront when a related news story broke. The result of this was what I call the expert sheet. An expert sheet is a simple release stating who the expert is and why. Credentials are important here so make sure and include those as well. Then, I keep them on file and whenever I see something in the news that relates to any one of my clients I quickly fax them over. Expert sheets don't have to be used solely for breaking news; they can also be used to stay in the forefront of any particular genre you are an expert in. For example, let's say your topic is childcare. You might want to send your expert sheet to all parenting related magazines on a monthly basis. That way, if they have a story in the queue they might consider contacting you. The format of an expert sheet should be no different from a press release except that at the top in big bold letters it should say "Expert Sheet" so it defines it immediately to whoever is receiving it. Keep in mind that an expert sheet should include two things: the tie-in and the expert's credentials. The media is very credential focused. They want to know whoever is being interviewed has the schooling or background to substantiate an interview.

Be Your Own Spy

When was the last time you monitored your competitor's Web sites, or even took a few minutes to look them over? If you don't, maybe you should. Get to know who else is out there sharing your "pond." Doing a periodic competitor check is a healthy way to stay in touch with other people in your industry and get to know the competition.

POSTCARDS

Imagination is more important than knowledge.
— Albert Einstein

One of the most important tools in my marketing package is a simple but stunning postcard. The front of the postcard is a copy of my book cover and the back can say whatever you want. The initial batch was printed with an announcement on the back heralding the arrival of *From Book to Bestseller*. Then, once that initial push was over, I had another batch printed with blank backs to use as thank you notes or whatever my little marketing heart desired. I would use these postcards for everything; I'd even have some special ones printed for book signings. The key here is consistency. You'll begin to develop a color scheme for your media package. I try to stay away from the formal and depressing black. Also, I would stick a copy of the postcard to the front of the folder and suddenly I had what looked like a very well thought-out and expensive kit. It was fun, colorful and informative.

Something I would also use the postcards for is to announce my media kit's arrival. Several days prior to the mailing, I would send out a postcard that said something like: Be on the lookout for your media kit, arriving shortly! Even if the postcard ended up in the circular file (and I'm sure many did) they would remember the cover of the book, and when it arrived, there would be an immediate sense of recognition. Even if the individual still had no idea what the book was about or if they even wanted to review it, they would remember it. In most cases, the announcement postcard was not the only form of advertising material they would receive from me. So again, when you're designing your marketing package, don't forget the all-important postcard. It's a vital and inexpensive part of your marketing campaign.

Marketing Tip

Don't ever send one single bit of correspondence without including a piece of marketing material, a bookmark or business card. Even include a bookmark when you pay your bills. Hey, your creditors always fill their envelopes with advertising, right? So why can't you?

One final marketing tidbit…did you know that contrary to popular belief it's the back of your postcard that gets the most attention, not the front? You have exactly three seconds to impress someone with whatever slogan or pitch before they'll turn the postcard over and look at the picture on the front.

Story of a Bestseller; The Power of a Postcard

If you question the power of sending a postcard, I hope this story will help you reconsider.

During the time I was promoting *The Cliffhanger*, the 2000 Presidential race was in progress. As it turned out, this event which could not have been further from the topic of my book, gave me the "hook" I needed to launch my book to the #1 bestselling spot on Amazon.com (bestselling book within San Diego).

Of course, how could *anyone* forget the questionable election that followed the Presidential race? How could you forget?! In the midst of chads, hanging and otherwise, our local paper ran a huge headline that read: Cliffhanger! I knew if I couldn't find a way to position my book around that, I needed to hang up my marketing hat. Problem: *The Cliffhanger* had *nothing* to do with politics. It was a love story about people in denial. (No news there.) Still, I knew if I looked hard enough, I could find a way.

I awoke that night at 3 a.m. with an idea so outrageous, I knew it had to work. I raced out to the office supply store the minute it opened to pick up several packs of clear labels. I got out the postcards I had printed with the book cover on them and attached labels with the following slogan:

Getting tired of the Presidential cliffhanger?

Try this one.

The Cliffhanger, a novel.

No politics involved.

I mailed 500 postcards out that day while praying the election wouldn't get called. I mailed these postcards to everyone in the media I'd ever contacted. Ever!

Days after my mass mailing, I was walking through my living room when suddenly I spotted my book cover on the screen. I was stunned. The local TV anchor was saying, "This has got to be the best thing I've ever seen. This lady wants you to go buy her book. I say everyone should rush out and buy it." And everyone did. That afternoon my book shot up to the #1 spot on Amazon where it stayed for three months. It even beat out Harry Potter, which was #4 at that time, yet Harry got the movie. Go figure.

That single postcard shot my book up the ranks at Amazon and quite literally changed my life and the way I look at marketing. To this day, people in the industry still know me as *The Cliffhanger* lady. And I'm happy and proud about that. It goes to show you that you never know what can happen from a single marketing effort. Sometimes nothing will come of it, and then other times you're watching TV and suddenly there's your book for the whole world to see!

SECTION THREE

BOOK REVIEWS

*There is no mistaking a real book when
one meets it. It is like falling in love.*
— Christopher Morley

LET'S REVIEW

*"Writing is like hunting. There are brutally cold afternoons
with nothing in sight, only the wind and your breaking
heart. Then the moment when you bag something big.
The entire process is beyond intoxicating."*
— *Kate Braverman*

It's a simple fact of life that people like what other people like. Book reviews feed right into this psychology. For this reason and several others, book reviews should be a vital part of your marketing campaign and should not be overlooked. Certainly, there's no such thing as free advertisement. Reviews however, come pretty close. For the cost of an advanced review copy or a book, you can garner a review (maybe several) that will begin to open doors for you. Even bad reviews can help you. I can even remember a little paper called *The New York Times* panning *Chicken Soup for the Soul* in a review. Didn't seem to hurt sales of that book, did it? You can't walk into a bookstore without seeing stacks and stacks of some sort of "Chicken Soup" book. There are so many editions now, I've lost count. So if you get a bad review, don't despair. Cash registers can still sing even if the review is negative.

Most first-time authors cannot afford to run ads in newspapers, nor should they. Buying ad space is largely ineffective and can come across as being gimmicky. An unbiased review can garner you media attention like nothing else, especially if you hit the big time with a larger publication.

Mail Tip!

Doing a mailing? Why not mail your mail on a Saturday to insure you get your mail into the hands of your recipient by Monday or Tuesday! Anything sent later in the week might be lost in the shuffle.

There are two types of reviews. The first of which is referred to as a pre-publication review. These reviewers will expect to see galley copies of your book. A galley copy is a printed copy of your book, neatly bound. If your galley still has typos in it or doesn't have an index yet, not to worry. Reviewers know they are advanced copies and expect that. There are several ways to produce galleys. If you're working with a publisher who is handling some of the reviews for you, they are probably producing galleys on your behalf. But, if you are self-publishing your book, you should be able to get galleys as part of your print run or, if your book is POD, you can use the initial copies you get of your book as galley versions. Book galleys are different because the cover isn't the final book cover. Instead, it's a cardstock cover with pertinent publication information on it. Here's a sample of one created for a book I worked on recently:

Uncorrected Proof
Advance Review Copy
For Limited Distribution Only

The Great California Story
Real-Life Roots of an American Legend

Carl Palm

Title:	The Great California Story
Subtitle:	Real-Life Roots of an American Legend
Author:	Carl Palm
Category:	History/ Popular Culture
ISBN:	1-59113-336-X (softcover)
ISBN:	1-59113-339-4 (hardcover)
Pub Date:	January 2006
Price:	$19.95 (softcover)
Price:	$32.95 (hardcover)
Pages:	380
Trim Size:	5.5" x 8.5"
Binding:	Perfect
Illustrated:	35 photographs, endnotes, and index
Backmatter:	Kevin Starr quote, summary, author
bioPublisher:	Northcross Books
Distribution:	Northcross, Ingram, Booklocker.com

Media Contact:
Penny C. Sansevieri
penny@amarketingexpert.com
(858) 560-0121

If you're working with a traditional galley (the card stock cover I just explained) then you'll want to include a color copy book cover sample. If you are working through a POD publisher, then you can get galleys printed separately but you don't have to. A book sent with the appropriate information should do the trick just as well. In fact, something I do when working with print-on-demand books is adhere a sticker to the front of the cover that states "Advanced Galley Copy." This tells the reviewer that I know they like advanced copies and I'm submitting mine in compliance with their guidelines. If you're doing it this way, I recommend that you get some labels and reprint the publication and contact information similar to the way a traditional galley cover is done and adhere it to the inside of the book. Invariably the media kit will get separated from your book and you want reviewers to have a way to contact you.

Now that your galley is ready, you're going to need to send it out to many, many reviewers.

Timing Is Everything

Believe it or not, the day your book arrives on the reviewer's desk can actually make a difference and even increase (or decrease) your chances for review. According to Jim Cox of *Midwest Book Review* (www.midwestbookreview. com),"Mondays are consistently the heaviest intake day for review copies. This is because UPS does not deliver on Saturday, and neither UPS nor the Post Office deliver on Sundays. So the books that are in UPS and Post Office pipelines over the weekend all show up added to the normal Monday intake. As the week progresses, the flow of books tends to die down a little, with Saturday, and only the Post Office delivering, tending to be the least numbers of books arriving. But countering that low Saturday figure is that while the book bags will be opened, it's fairly frequent that the books themselves will simply be stacked and added to the Monday piles before starting through the process of examination to determine their status with respect to the review selection routine." That said, the two best days for your book to arrive on a reviewer's desk are Thursday or Friday. The competition of your book's arriving decreases as the week progresses. There's really no way to ensure that the Post Office will deliver when you hope unless you get three day, or overnight delivery. If you're not sure about the time frame for delivery these days, have the tracking feature added to a few of your packages to see when they arrive. Generally, January and February tend to be the best months for submitting your book for review. According to Jim Cox, avoid sending these October & November, which are peak promotional months for major publishers. The second worst months are April & May. This is because they're the "hump months" for the Spring Season releases for the big guys who have distinct Spring & Fall Seasons to their marketing. Besides January and February, the best months or, "slump months" as most reviewers refer to them as, are March, June, July & August.

Marketing Tip

If you're sending review copies, I'd advise you not to mail these between the days of November 15th through December 27th as they might instead wind up as holiday gifts and never get reviewed.

Library reviews

We've included some major library reviewers in the reviewer list that follows. Why? Because getting your book into a library is a major coup for your marketing campaign. According to Book Industry Trends 2001, libraries spent over $4.2 billion on books, periodicals, audiovisuals, and other related materials in 2000. Nearly $2 million of that was spent on book purchases.

Review Packets

When submitting materials for review, your review packet should contain materials pertaining to your book only; this is not a pitch packet so they will be decidedly different. Review packets need to contain the following information:

- Well-worded letter to your intended reviewer: Remember that you need to "sell" them on your book so make this letter as intriguing as you can!

- Bio sheet: This is where you include the bio sheet created for your press kit.

- Press release: This should be a general release; it does not need to tie into a current event. This release should focus on your book.

- Marketing objectives: Often I will include a short (one paragraph) summary of the marketing plans for this book. Even a bullet point list will do. It doesn't need to be extensive; the reviewer will simply want to see that you've outlined a plan.

- Review sheet: This sheet is a one-page overview listing all the pertinent info related to your book. Here's a sample of what this sheet should look like:

The Great California Story

Full title:	The Great California Story; *Real-Life Roots of an American Legend*
Author:	Carl Palm
Publisher:	Northcross Books
Release Date:	January 2006
Category:	History/Popular Culture
ISBN:	1-59113-336 X (softcover) 1-59113-339-4 (hardcover)
Formats/editions:	Paperback Hardcover
Price:	$19.95 (softcover) $32.95 (hardcover)

Please mail a copy of the review to:

Penny C. Sansevieri
Author Marketing Experts, Inc.
Post Office Box 421156
San Diego, CA 92142

Your advanced copies should go to the following reviewers:

Prepublication Date Reviewers

ALA Booklist

Up Front, Advance Reviews

50 East Huron Street

Chicago, Illinois 60611

http://www.ala.org/ala/booklist/booklist.htm

Due to the volume of submissions (more than 60,000 per year), Booklist is unable to notify authors or publishers whose books have not been selected for review. Any author or publisher whose book has been selected for review will receive a tear sheet of the review. All submissions of materials for review become the sole property of the American Library Association; request for return of materials or other restrictions cannot be honored.

There are specific Book Review Editors you'll need to target, here's the list they'd like you to work from:

Adult Books: Brad Hooper, Adult Books Editor

Books for Youth (Children's and YA): Stephanie Zvirin, Books for Youth Editor

Reference Books: Mary Ellen Quinn, *Reference Books Bulletin* Editor

ForeWord Magazine
Alex Moore Book Review Editor
129 1/2 East Front Street
Traverse City, MI 49684

www.forewordmagazine.com
E-mail: Reviews@foreword.com
Phone: (231) 933-3699

ForeWord Magazine is a monthly trade review journal covering independent and university presses that provides a news and review vehicle for booksellers, librarians and publishing professionals. Of the 500+ books the magazine receives each month, the editors select 40–60 for review. Books chosen for pre-publication review by Review Editor Alex Moore represent the season's most worthy materials. The choices range from original paperbacks, hardcover, audio and electronic books. Books are selected for their potential interest to a trade buying audience. About 40% of *ForeWord* subscribers are acquisition directors at libraries; about 40% of readers are trade booksellers, encompassing chain and independent retail outlets; and another 20% are in the industry, including publishers, agents, and association professionals. *ForeWord* reviews are used by booksellers and librarians to make purchasing decisions from the universe of independently published materials flooding the marketplace. *ForeWord* does not review textbooks, technical or specialized works (particularly those directed at a professional audience), or books in languages other than English. They do consider bilingual editions and books previously published abroad if they are being released here for the first time and have a U.S. distributor. Materials must be sent three to four months in advance of publication date to be considered for review or mention. Galleys are suitable materials to send. *ForeWord* generally avoids reviewing books later than date of publication, though they do make exceptions for children's and audio books. Authors who want to know if their submissions have been received should e-mail reviews@forewordmagazine.com a few

days after their estimated day of arrival. To find out if a book
is going to be reviewed, e-mail reviews@forewordmagazine.
com 45 days after the submission's arrival.

Library Journal
Book Review Editor
360 Park Avenue South
New York, New York
www.libraryjournal.com/index.asp?layout=forReviewersLJ
Phone: (212) 463-6818
Fax: (212) 463-6734

The Library Journal is a magazine geared to public libraries.
Of the 30,000 books they receive, they will usually review
4,500 each year. A good review by The LJ might move between
1,000 to 5,000 copies of your book. Books are selected for their
potential interest to a broad spectrum of libraries. About 60%
of The LJ's readers are in public libraries; another 21% are in
academic libraries; about 13% are in special libraries; and about
6% are in school libraries. Their reviews are used primarily by
librarians to make their purchasing decisions. Only a few areas
of publishing fall outside LJ's scope: textbooks, children's
books, very technical or specialized works (particularly those
directed at a professional audience), and books in languages
other than English. They will consider bilingual editions, and
have a quarterly review of Spanish-language books. Books
previously published abroad are eligible if they are being
released here for the first time and have a U.S. distributor.
Recently, *The Library Journal* has begun accepting print-on-
demand books. This came directly from their Web site: "We do
consider print-on-demand and online materials, but we would

like to see these materials as much in advance of the launch date as possible. For print-on-demand books, please send us proofs as soon as they are available and specify estimated launch date as well as ISBN, price, and other relevant material, as with any traditional book. Include the following information: Author, title; name, address, and telephone number of publisher; date of publication; price; number of pages; and ISBN and LC numbers if available. Please indicate whether any illustrations, an index, or bibliography will be included; also include a brief description of the book, its intended audience, and information on the author's background."

New York Times Sunday Book Reviews
Sam Tanenhaus, Editor
229 W. 43rd St.
New York, NY 10036
bookreview@nytimes.com
Phone: (212) 556-1466
Fax: (212) 556-3815

Send galleys two to three months prior to your pub date. Send a finished copy of the book once it's available.

The Village Voice
Ed Park, Book Reviews Senior Editor
36 Cooper Square
New York, NY 10003
epark@villagevoice.com
Phone: (212) 475-3300 Ext. 12208
Fax: (212) 475-8944

The Village Voice considers reviews for literary fiction and literary, illustrated, political, and topical nonfiction. They rarely but occasionally review genre fiction and children's literature; they almost never review self-help or business books. Take a look at recent issues (you can read them online at www.villagevoice. com) and determine whether your book seems appropriate for their section. They prefer to receive galleys at least two months before the publication date. If that isn't possible, or if galleys aren't available, send them the finished book, along with a press release containing any pertinent information. They also say that fancy press kits and author photos aren't necessary and won't impact their decision–making process.

If you have a New York reading in the near future, send a press release at least two weeks beforehand to: Grace Bastidas, Listings Department (see address above). You can also fax press releases on readings to Bastidas at (212) 475-5807.

As with most reviewers, don't call the Voice repeatedly and ask whether they received your book or press release, and whether they know yet what issue you'll be reviewed in. If you sent it, the odds are pretty good they received it. The odds are also good that, since they get about 200 books every week, they haven't read it yet. But they do promise to make the effort to look at every book and press release they receive. If they review your book in the book section or the literary supplement, they will send you a copy of the review once it appears. If you want to double check if your book has been reviewed, you can also go to www.villagevoice.com, and type your name into the search engine. Maybe you'll be surprised.

Chicago Tribune Books
Elizabeth Taylor
435 N. Michigan Avenue
Chicago, IL 60611
http://www.chicagotribune.com/entertainment/arts/
Phone: (312) 222-3232
E-mail: etaylor@tribune.com

The *Chicago Tribune* reviews galleys two to three months prior to the publication date. Once your book rolls off the presses you'll want to send them a finished copy of that as well. Elizabeth is very busy and you should only e-mail to check receipt of the book or for some other important (and relevant) issue.

The American Book Review
Charles Harris, Publisher
Illinois State University Campus
Box 4241
Normal, IL 61790-0001
Phone: (309) 438-2127
Fax: (309) 438-3523

The American Book Review is an internationally circulated bimonthly print journal that specializes in reviews of frequently neglected published works of fiction, poetry, and literary criticism from small, regional, university, ethnic, avant-garde, and women's presses. ABR as a literary journal aims to project the sense of engagement that writers themselves feel about what is being published.

They do not review non-literary works, which includes such subjects as self-help, health, or how-to. You may send all review copies (galleys are fine). They will consider books within six months of their publication dates. Follow-up inquiries can be made to the e-mail address listed above.

Ruminator Review
Margaret Todd Maitland, Editor
1648 Grand Avenue
St. Paul, MN 55105
www.ruminator.com
Phone: (651) 699-2610
Fax: (651) 699-0970
E-mail: review@hungrymind.com

The *Ruminator Review* will accept galleys or final copies three to four months prior to the pub date. The magazine is sent quarterly to 30,000 subscribers and sold in 350 bookstores.

Romantic Times Magazine
Small Press Reviewer
55 Bergen Street
Brooklyn, NY 11201
www.romantictimes.com
Phone: (718) 237-1097
E-mail: rtinfo@romantictimes.com

Romantic Times Magazine will only review galleys. Besides romance they also review mystery and science fiction novels.

Rain Taxi
PO Box 3840
Minneapolis, MN 55403
www.raintaxi.com

Winner of the 2000 Alternative Press Award for Best Arts and Literature Coverage, the quarterly *Rain Taxi Review of Books* provides a place for the spirited exchange of ideas about books, particularly those overlooked by mainstream review media.

Rain Taxi considers books in the categories of poetry, fiction, and literary non-fiction (such as biography, philosophy, or cultural studies). They also regularly review graphic novels and audio publications (CDs). They do not review books in other areas (e.g., gardening, cooking, business, self-help...) unless there is a significant literary connection. They will occasionally review children's books.

Please note that only finished books or bound galleys are accepted for consideration.

Because of the volume of books they receive, *Rain Taxi* asked that you not contact them to follow up. If your book is selected for review you will be contacted.

If you're thinking of placing an ad instead of sending your book in for review consider this. Only 3% of books were purchased from ads placed in magazines or newspapers.

Post-Publication Date Reviewers

Once your book has rolled off of the presses, it's time to send out more review copies. I recommend sending a copy of the book along with a media kit.

Midwest Book Review
James A. Cox, Editor-in-Chief
278 Orchard Drive
Oregon, WI 53575
http://www.midwestbookreview.com/
Phone: (608) 835-7937

Midwest Book Review reviews approximately 450 books each month out of the 1,500 they receive. James Cox says they will consider any book as long as it's in finished form. Send a copy of your book and press release. He says he prefers not getting an entire media kit.

Amazon Book Reviews
Editorial Department
Post Office Box 81226
Seattle, WA 98108-1226
www.amazon.com
Phone: (206) 266-2952

They prefer finished copies, but I'd call and check with them to find out specific departments to address this to, based on your genre. They are revising this process as of this writing, so it's best to check with them to get the most current information.

USA Today
Carol Memmott, Book Editor
7950 Jones Branch Drive
McLean, VA 22107
www.usatoday.com
(703) 276-3400

A finished book should be sent to them one month before the pub date.

LA Times Book Magazine
David Ulin, Book Reviews Editor
202 W 1st St
Los Angeles, CA 90012-4105
Phone: (213) 237-7778
Fax: (213) 237-4712
www.latimes.com
david.ulin@latimes.com

Send finished books no further out than three months past the pub date.

New York Review of Books
Robert Silvers
1755 Broadway, Floor 5
New York, NY 10019
www.nybooks.com
Phone: (212) 757-8070
Fax: (212) 333-5374

New York Review of Books accepts finished books only. Not too far from the pub date is always preferred. This is a biweekly magazine that publishes reviews, excerpts, and will also buy serial rights. Their circulation is 130,000 and they review 400 books each year.

The Boox Review
Geoff Rotunno
Managing Director
P.O. Box 211
Santa Ynez, CA 93460
www.thebooxreview.com

Send them finished books, no further than three months past the publication date.

Denise Hill, Editor
NewPages
PO Box 1580
Bay City, MI 48706
www.newpages.com

Send them finished books, no further than three months past the publication date.

Book Passage
Elaine Petrocelli
Book Passage News & Reviews
51 Tamal Vista Blvd
Corte Madera, CA 94925
www.bookpassage.com
Send them finished books, no further than three months past the publication date

The Bloomsbury Review
1553 Platte Street, Suite 206
Denver, CO 80202-1167 USA
www.bloomsburyreview.com
Phone: (303) 455-3123
Fax: (303) 455-7039
E-mail: info@bloomsburyreview.com

Send them finished books, no further than three months past the publication date.

Writers Write, Inc.
Attention: Reviews
8214 Westchester Suite 500
Dallas, TX 75225
www.writerswrite.com

Send them finished books, no further than three months past the publication date

How to make sure your book doesn't fall into the black hole of book reviews:

Find out what the submission guidelines are and follow them. When in doubt, ask!

Is your book right for this publication?

Do they do book reviews?

Try tying your submission to a particular time of the year.

When appropriate, do a 10-day follow up to make sure your book has been received and whether or not it's been assigned to a reviewer.

Online Review Sites:

- Bookreporter.com (www.bookreporter.com) If you use this one, you might want to note they do not review print-on-demand, how-to, business, self help, spiritual and religious books
- Bookbrowse.com (www.bookbrowse.com)
- Bookideas.com (www.bookideas.com)
- Book Review Café (www.bookreviewcafe.com)
- Book Pleasures (www.bookpleasures.com/Lore2/)
- Critique Magazine (www.critiquemagazine.com)
- Curled Up With a Good Book (www.curledup.com)
- Myshelf.com (www.myshelf.com)
- Rawsistaz Book Club (www.rawsistaz.com)
- List of Book Reviewers (www.geocities.com/ladyjiraff/reviewers.html)
- Book Fetish (www.bookfetish.com)
- Armchair Interviews (www.armchairinterviews.com)
- Reader Views (www.readerviews.com)

Looking for even more places to send your book for review? Pick up a copy of *The Self Publishing Manual* by Dan Poynter or check out his Web site at <u>www.parapublishing.com</u>.

NICHE REVIEWS

If a window of opportunity appears,
don't pull down the shade.
— *Tom Peters*

Besides the standard review markets, you might want to consider garnering more niche reviews. Once you've figured out who your specific audience is, you can target your book for niche reviews. For example, is your book on European travel? Check the travel section of your local paper and see if there's a spot for your book. In my Sunday paper there is a whole travel section complete with travel advice and articles (hint, hint). There are hundreds of syndicated columnists, reporters and editors that have newspaper space to fill. Several years ago I was working on getting reviews for *A Dance in the Desert*, a book about one man's struggle with epilepsy. Given the subject of the book, I went to national epilepsy foundations and asked if they would review the book for their newsletters and magazines. In so doing, I captured an audience either directly or indirectly affected by this disease who were interested in the author's book. Find out who your audience is, then study the various publications and target them for a copy of your book. If you're looking for a list of syndicated columnists nationwide, try *Editor & Publisher*. They do an issue in August that classifies columnists by subject matter. The cost for this is $8.50 and can be obtained by checking out their Web site at www.editorandpublisher.com, or by calling (212) 675-4380

Now, what about the magazine market? When I began to research this market I was astounded to find out how many different magazines there were that I had never even heard of. Did you write something on the mining industry? How about contacting someone at Coal Age to see if they're interested in looking at your book? Is your book animal related? How about Reptile Fancy or Ferret Fancy (by the same company that does Cat Fancy)? See what I mean? Get on your browser and type in "magazine" you'll be amazed at what comes up.

More Directories and Alternative Review Sources:

QBR: The Black Book Review
Max Rodriguez, Publisher
9 West 126th Street, 2nd Floor
New York, NY 10027
www.qbr.com
Phone: (212) 348-1681
Fax: (212) 427-9901.
mrodz@qbr.com

This review of African American books is published six times per year.

Books & Culture: A Christian Book Review
John Wilson, Editor
465 Gundersen Drive
Carol Stream IL 60188
www.christianitytoday.com
Phone: (630) 260-6200
Fax: (630) 260-0114.

This bimonthly magazine reviews books on science, politics, culture, fiction, etc. from a Christian perspective. Circulation: 16,000.

New Age Retailer
Continuity Publishing
Kathy McGee, Editor in Chief
2183 Alpine Way
Bellingham,. WA 98226
Phone: (360) 676-0789
Fax: (360) 676-0932
E-mail: mail@ newageretailer.com.

Travel Books Worldwide
Peter Manston, Editor
2510 S Street, P.O. Box 162266
Sacramento, CA 95816-2266
Phone: (916) 452-5200

Black Issues Book Review
Clarence V. Reynolds, Managing Editor
Empire State Building
350 Fifth Avenue Suite 1522
New York, NY 10118
www.bibookreview.com
Phone: (212) 947-8515
Fax: (212) 947-5674.
E-mail: bibredit@cmapublishing

Science Fiction Chronicle
Donald Dammassa, Book Reviewer
323 Dodge St.
East Providence, RI 0291

Phone: (718) 643-9011
Fax: (718) 522-3308
E-mail: sf_chronicle@compuserve.com

Sci/Tech Book News
Jane Erskine, Managing Editor
5739 N.E. Sumner Street
Portland, OR 97218
www.dnapublications.com/revs/amrevcur.htm
Phone: (503) 281- 9230
Fax: (503) 287-4485
E-mail: booknews@ booknews.com

Association of Alternative News Weeklies
1250 Eye Street, N.W., Suite 804
Washington, D.C. 20005
Phone: (202) 289-8484
Fax: (202) 289-2004
E-mail: web@aan.org

These sites are courtesy of John Kremer. Need more review sites? Take a look at John Kremer's Web site at www.bookmarket.com and click on major newspaper book reviewers.

Mock Reviews

Remember the Golden Rule of media: Make their life as easy as you can! This includes slipping a mock review into your media kit. It may seem counterintuitive to write your own review but it's done and it often helps the reviewers jump-start their own thoughts. Put together a flattering blurb about your book and include it in your package. Many times, the reviewer will end up using what you've already written or excerpting portions of it for his or her own review.

Following Up

After 10 days to two weeks, follow up with the reviewer to see if your book has been selected for review. Keep this conversation brief and know that you might be making the same call 10 times until you get an answer. First, you want to introduce yourself and let them know you are calling to confirm that they received your book (mention the title). If they say they haven't received it, offer to call back in a week. Reviewers often get five crates of books to review each day. As you can imagine, this takes a while to sift through. If the reviewer has received your book, ask him or her what the status is with regard to the review process. If they tell you that it has been selected for review, inquire as to when a review could be expected, and check to see if there is anything else they require from you. Thank them before hanging up. If it has not yet been scheduled for review, ask them if there is anything else they need to make their decision. Suggest calling them back in a week or two (get the best day and time to call), thank them and hang up. Don't keep them on the phone with pressing questions about their time frame. Do take copious notes and keep a log handy of when you called and what transpired during the contact. Each time you phone a reviewer you need to sound fresh, happy and accommodating to their needs. If the book isn't right for them or they won't review it for whatever reason, thank them politely and move on to your next reviewer.

A Final Word on Reviews

Rarely will someone perusing a book on Amazon buy something "naked." Now, we're not referring to what you're wearing when you shop but rather, the book page itself. Unless you've gone to the site specifically to purchase that book, consumers will rarely buy something that doesn't have a single review. That's why I encourage you to do whatever you can to dress up your page. This means encouraging anyone and everyone who has computer access to review your book on the Amazon and Barnes & Noble Web sites. If you have a newsletter or mailing list, you might put out an offer of a second book discounted (or free) just for posting a review (good or bad) of your book. If you do give a book for your reader to give away, see about getting the name of the person they gave it to, or better yet, mail it to them yourself and extend this offer to them as well.

Another way to garner reviews is to review books in your category or genre (you are reading the competition, aren't you?). Register yourself with Amazon before you review someone else's book. When you do this and post a review it will refer people to the "see more about me" page, which will be your book. If the consumer was already interested in the competition, they will probably want your book too. So you're not only helping out the competition with a review, but driving traffic to your book as well!

SECTION FOUR

OUTSIDE THE BOOK MARKETING STRATEGIES

*The role of a writer is not to say what we
all can say, but what we are unable to say.*
— Anaïs Nin

THINKING OUTSIDE THE BOOKSTORE BOX!

A bookstore is one of the only pieces of evidence
we have that people are still thinking.
— *Jerry Seinfeld*

When I was first published, like my authors, one of my all-time aspirations was to see my book in a bookstore window. I soon found out that the competition for bookstore shelf space was fierce. I was up against the likes of Dean Koontz, Nora Roberts, and Dan Brown. But after speaking with many small publishers, I knew I wasn't alone. The fact of the matter is, large publishing houses will actually purchase space on bookstore shelves thereby virtually guaranteeing them a spot. Next time you walk through a bookstore, take a look at the placement of books. Have you ever wondered why some books end up on the promotions table right as you're walking through the door? Or why some get front row exposure on end-caps? It's not because some nice salesperson put them there. It's because a publisher bought space in those areas. This doesn't mean that you won't ever get your book into stores; you will probably succeed in placing them locally. As far as nationwide exposure goes though, that probably won't come until you've built some momentum for your book. If statistics are any guide though, it's fair to say that bookstores aren't the only ticket in town. In fact, according to the Book Industry Study Group (BISG), bookstores accounted for 35% of retail sales in the United States in 1998; the remaining 65% of the retail market is now divided among mass-market retailers, mail order, book clubs, specialty stores, and online booksellers. This means that even though bookstores seem like the logical place to carry your book, most people who have reached success have done so by thinking outside the bookstore box. Consider for a moment the potential of online sales. A report recently released by Cambridge, Massachusetts-based Forrester Research ("U.S. eCommerce Overview: 2003 to 2008") indicates that online retail book sales will nearly double over the next five years. The study further indicated that online sales will account for 10 % of total U.S. retail sales by 2008.

Staggering Statistics

- 7% of the books published generated 87% of total retail bookstore sales.

- 1,187 titles sold 50,000 or more copies.

- 24,000 books had sales of over 5,000 units.

- 93% of all books published sold less than 1,000 copies.

    (Source: Book Industry Study Group)

Take a closer look at non-traditional markets. Thinking small or niche might seem odd, but it's very effective. Isolate your target market as I discussed in "Who's Your Market" and go after that target audience. Self-published or small press authors don't have the advantage of a large marketing budget so they must make certain each promotional effort is targeted. Being creative is an important thing for *any* author to do.

Before he became a best-selling author, E. Lynn Harris left copies of his self-published books in beauty salons. Why beauty salons? Because at the salon people have a lot of time to read. He had a built-in audience and was able to cultivate a loyal following. That's creative (and smart) marketing. Jim Donovan, author of *Handbook to a Happier Life*, struggled with the same challenge when he was marketing his book. "I decided to approach a pet store that I frequented to see if they would carry the book." Donovan. said. Since his book was not animal related, I asked him, why a pet store? His answer was simple: "I have no competition." The book is displayed at the register and does very well. "Don't get caught up in bookstore sales," says Donovan, "most of the American population has never even been in a bookstore." Give some thought for a moment as to where else you might see books. How about a museum, an amusement park, or even a national park? What about office supply stores, gas stations, travel stores, empowerment stores (Successories), record stores, wineries, children's stores, home stores, day spas or beauty salons, novelty shops, kitchen and cooking stores (Williams-Sonoma)? Get the picture? There are hundreds upon hundreds of alternative spots to carry your book. These are only just a few. I'm certain you can think of many more.

Did you know?

A new Barnes and Noble store typically opens with 100,000 new titles. How will your reader find yours?

Now, this doesn't mean you should ignore the bookstore idea altogether. As a matter of fact, when you're out and about you should always make it a point to drop into any bookstore you run across. Introduce yourself to the store manager or community relations manager and hand them a copy of your book. It's even more impressive if you have a press kit already made up, as well. Even if you don't have a copy of your book with you (shame on you) make sure to carry some business cards, bookmarks or postcards. Don't even think of going in there without leaving something behind! You should get to know your area bookstores and offer to come in there and sign books, do a reading or host a seminar. Give them something to give their customers. Even if they can't stock your book in their store, they might consider hosting a signing anyway, just to support a local writer. Most bookstores are very good about supporting their community. And if they're not interested right away (their event calendars fill up very quickly), they might be interested later on down the road, so make sure to keep in touch with them.

Did you know?

The five reasons people buy in bookstores:

- Reviews, publicity

- Recommendations

- Browsing

- Window displays, end-caps or face-out books

- Staff recommendations

BOOK CLUBS

There are three rules for writing a novel.
Unfortunately, no one knows what they are.
— F. Somerset Maugham

Getting into a book club means the kind of exposure you can't get anywhere else. If you've ever belonged to a book club, you know that they send you a catalog each month and you have to send back their form if you don't want the selection of the month. Otherwise, it's automatically sent to you. Whoever came up with this idea was brilliant!

In days-gone-by, book clubs were the ideal way to reach people in remote areas or avid readers too busy to spend an afternoon in a bookstore. Book clubs were made attractive with deals, bonus points, and free books just for signing up. But with the advent of the Internet, all of that is beginning to change. First of all, online bookstores like Barnes & Noble and Amazon are the solution to those unable to get to the bookstore; they can shop in their bunny slippers. The Internet has also, in a sense, raised the bar on offers, pricing and service. Book clubs are going online now so members don't have to hassle with envelopes and postage. And if you've ever been a member of a book club you know that customer service was probably the last thing on their list. Well, not anymore. The Net has forced them to be more responsive, and in a sense, breathed new life into these American institutions.

In March of 2000, the nation's two oldest book clubs joined forces. Book of the Month Club and The Literary Guild, once arch rivals competing over deals, authors and books, were now on the same team and Bookspan was born. This partnership encompasses more than 40 clubs with access to 10 million active members. President and CEO, Markus Wilhelm, believes that in the next couple of years they could be looking at over 100 clubs total. A study done by polling and trend group Roper ASW concluded that book clubs are the best source for helping readers decide what books to purchase as a result of seeing a book club advertisement or monthly mailing. In fact, about six in 10 customers have purchased a book in a store or online as a result of seeing a book club advertisement or monthly mailing.

In 2003, Bookspan announced its first international book club. Given this history, you can imagine that going forward, the doors will open for a variety of new clubs and catalogs. Imagine what this could mean for book sales.

Guidelines for clubs are simple. Send them a copy of your manuscript well in advance of your publication date. In fact, they invite you to submit manuscripts six to 10 months out, as they would rather have a typescript early than a set of bound galleys or a finished book late. Tardy submissions have a reduced chance of adoption. According to some recently updated information, they buy from both traditional houses and small presses. In fact, they welcome small press submissions and love discovering exciting new authors. Submit your sample to them along with a cover letter indicating the estimated pub date, book price, page count, a brief description of the book, summary of its content, and the number and type of illustrations. It's also helpful to send photocopies of sample illustrations and an author bio noting any previous books. Package all of this up, and send it to the book club that you feel best fits your audience.

Bookspan
15 East 26th St.
New York, NY 10010
www.bookspan.com
Phone (212) 651-7400

When you visit the Bookspan Web site, click on "Business Opportunities" and then "Submitting Manuscripts" for an updated listing of their editors and submission process. You can also surf through their Web site to see if they've added any new clubs to their Bookspan family.

The following clubs are all part of the Bookspan group and have the same mailing address. Make sure and address it to "Editorial Department" and mark the name of the book club you're targeting clearly on the package.

Here is a current list of their clubs. I recommend that before submitting your book to a particular club you check their Web site to confirm the club is still active or if another, possibly more appropriate club, has been added:

- Architects & Designers Book Service

- Behavioral Science Book Club

- Black Expressions Book Club

- Book-of-the-Month Club

- Children's Book-of-the-Month Club

- Computer Books Direct Book Club
- Country Homes & Gardens Book Club
- Crafter's Choice Book Club
- Discovery Channel Book Club
- Doubleday Book Club
- Doubleday Large Print Book Club
- Early Childhood Teachers Book Club
- Equestrian Book Club
- The Good Cook Book Club
- History Book Club
- Intermediate & Middle Grades Book Club
- Library of Science Book Club
- The Library of Speech-Language Pathology
- The Literary Guild
- The Military Book Club
- Mystery Guild
- One Spirit Book Club
- Outdoorsman's Edge Book Club
- Nurse's Book Society
- Primary Teachers' Book Club
- Quality Paperback Book Club
- Reader's Subscription Book Club
- Rhapsody Book Club
- Science Fiction Book Club

Got Books?

Last year, I got 100 copies of my book, *The Cliffhanger*, with misprinted covers. I couldn't resell them, so they sat boxed up in my office. I tried organizing a book signing for charity but the idea never got off the ground. I was finally referred to The Friends of the Library. They take used books and resell them and the proceeds benefit your local library. Some are even given to the homeless. What a great cause! If you have some books you need to get rid of, don't hang onto them the way I did – get in touch with your local branch of Friends of the Library and donate them. And, if you're interested in finding a great sale on used books, head on over to www.booksalefinder. com. This site lists all library-related sale events in your area.

Alternative Book Clubs

Even though Bookspan is the largest, it's by no means the only book club. Both online and off, book clubs are big business and a great way to spread the word about your book. One such club, DearReader.com (www.dearreader.com), began with an interesting concept. They feature a new selection Monday through Friday with book club members receiving a 5-minute book sample delivered directly to their e-mail. The reads are consecutive, giving the reader a chance to get "hooked" on the book they are previewing. They offer 11 different clubs in total: fiction, nonfiction, romance, audio, teen, business, mystery, good news (features Christian titles), horror, sci-fi, and prepublications (books featured a few weeks before their release date). As of this writing, DearReader.com boasts over 220,000 members and this list is growing everyday.

To submit a book to them for consideration send your advanced copy or final book to:

DearReader.com
1002 S. Orange Ave.
Sarasota, FL 34236

Be sure to put your contact information in the book. This is important so that the staff at DearReader.com can notify you that your book has been selected. They do not accept poetry books, or books comprised of short stories. Also, keep in mind that they preview only 8,500 words, or about the first 23 pages of your book. If that number of pages is more than 10 percent of your total book, then the selection probably isn't right for the club.

———

If you'd like to find out about more book clubs here are two more sites you can check out: www.book-clubs.com and www.allbookstores.com/bookclubs.

———

Local Book Clubs

If you scour your local area, I bet you'll find quite a few book clubs that meet in person on a regular basis. But how to find them? Well, try going to your local bookstore and talking to the manager. They will probably be able to tell you whether they have an in-store club, and if they don't, they can probably direct you to one locally. When you get this information, find out who is the group coordinator. Contact them to see if you can offer your book as a possible book selection or, if the club has speakers, see if they'll let you do a reading at one of their next meetings. If you think local book clubs are a waste of your time consider this: *The Divine Secrets of the Ya-Ya Sisterhood* tanked when it was first released. It wasn't until a few local book groups got a hold of this book that it flourished and eventually hit the bestseller lists!

If You Love Your Book, Set it Free.

That's the motto at Book Crossing (www.bookcrossing.com), now boasting several million members worldwide. They have a unique concept; read a book, then release it. They call it the book club that knows no boundaries. You'll give your newly freed book a tracking number and label so you can follow your book on its journey around the globe. I try to release one book a month this way, it's a great way to spread the word about your book – but does it sell books? You betcha. Since readers are encouraged to re-release the books, they find if they want a personal copy of the book they read through the Book Crossing system that – guess what? -- they have to buy it. So read and release. It's not only a great way to share your book with the world but it's just good book karma.

Did You Know?

The top 10 most literate cities, according to a CCSU study, are:

1. Seattle, Washington
2. Minneapolis, Minnesota
3. Washington, D.C.
4. Atlanta, Georgia
5. San Francisco, California
6. Denver, Colorado
7. Boston, Massachusetts
8. Pittsburgh, Pennsylvania
9. Cincinnati, Ohio
10. St Paul, Michigan

So which ones ranked at the bottom? The answer might surprise you:

1. Riverside, CA
2. Los Angeles, CA
3. Long Beach, CA
4. Santa Ana, CA
5. Fresno CA
6. San Antonio, TX
7. Bakersfield, CA
8. Anaheim, CA

9. Corpus Christi, Texas

10. El Paso, Texas

So which city ranked the least (of all) literate places in the US? Stockton, CA.

From the Central Connecticut State University study of "America's Most Literate Cities" by Dr. John W. Miller. The study was done in 2005 (www.ccsu.edu/amlc/)

COURTING SPECIAL SALES

"I am the world's worst salesman, therefore,
I must make it easy for people to buy."
— F. W. Woolworth

Have you ever dreamed of selling your book to a large corporation? A sale that would potentially register several thousand copies of non-returnable product on the book sale meter? What's that? You've never thought of it you say? Well, never fear! It's not too late to pursue this avenue, especially if you have a book ripe for a particular market.

Before you embark on this project, it's important to understand the possibilities out there. Start being aware of incentive items you might see and understand how they are used. Many are offered as consumer gifts or incentives while others are used as training tools or morale boosters for employees.

Some examples of special (or premium) sales might be:

• Books offered at yearly company sales meetings

• Books offered to consumers at a discount (consumers are usually asked to send in product UPC's to qualify for these specials)

• Books offered to new customers at financial institutions

- Books offered to new home buyers

- Books offered to new magazine subscribers

To determine the market segment you want to go after, study your book first for obvious clues. If you've mentioned or recommended companies or products in your book, those will be the first tier you'll want to go after. Next, think about the message of your book and how it aligns with particular companies within that industry. Company Web sites and ads will offer great clues when trying to match a company or organization up with your book.

If you're going after the magazine subscriber bonus segment, you'll have a bit more flexibility. Generally, if the book fits the reader demographic and aligns itself with the message of the magazine, it will be considered. For example, you might offer a home organization book to *Good Housekeeping* or a fitness book to *Self* or *Shape*. Before you approach these magazines, read them for about three months so you get a good sense of what they're about and who their audience is.

If you're going after a particular market and are trying to locate companies within that industry, try doing a Boolean search in Google. Your search should look like this: "your industry and companies." Another resource is www.thomasnet. com/index.html. This site will link you to companies nationally and internationally within your industry.

Next, don't overlook companies in your own backyard. Think about industries, companies and organizations in your area that might work well for your book and begin going after them. Many times, local companies will welcome the opportunity to support hometown authors.

Once you've put your list together, you'll want to contact them and pitch them the idea. Or, in some cases, my company will send them the book and proposal before we even make phone contact. Sometimes the companies you've targeted will be on the lookout for incentive items, other times this will be a new, and exciting, area for them. If you're going after employee incentives, it's interesting to note (and mention in your sales letter) that employee incentives increase individual performance by 27 percent and team performance by 45 percent.

Be open and creative with your pursuit of special or premium sales! Many times, companies will want to put their logo on the cover or include an extra page in the book with a letter from the President or CEO. Check with your printer or publisher on whether this is possible for you and what the additional costs will be before you start pursuing the special sales arena.

So, how long does this process take? We've seen some special or premium sales turn around in a week, while others take a year or more to complete. Oh, and the most important part... how many books can you plan to sell? Anywhere from 1,000 to several thousand depending on the deal and the company. We've even got a deal in the works for a half a million copies of one book. Discounts and negotiations vary. Often, we'll negotiate volume discounts of 50 percent to 70 percent on bulk orders. Again, make sure you've got these figures ready when you pick up the phone to make your pitch.

With the right book, premium sales are not only a great way to gain exposure for your book, but in the end, they make great "cents."

Is Your Book Ready for College?

I was sitting beside a college professor on a flight and we began discussing books and education. He said that often a professor will assign his own book as reading material to the class. But, he indicated, colleges are always open to considering new titles and are very open to suggestion. If your book is appropriate to this market why not suggest it?

Selling to Staples

Have you been to your local Staples store recently? If you have you've probably seen how they've expanded their book section. If you think your book is perfect for their store, shoot them an e-mail at newproducts@staples.com to get their new product submission form. Don't forget to put "new product submission" in the subject line!

GETTING YOUR BOOK ON QVC

There is no chance, no destiny, no fate, that can hinder or control the firm resolve of a determined soul.
— *Ella Wheeler Wilcox*

If you've ever channel-surfed your way to QVC you've probably experienced the QVC "buzz" firsthand. You don't watch QVC as a rule but for some reason, you can't seem to switch the channel once you're there. It's engaging, fun, and dare I say, even a bit exciting. As the time ticks by with only seconds left to sell a product, you feel so compelled to buy it you're already reaching for the phone when the smiling host says: "Sorry folks, we just sold out." And suddenly you feel like you just missed out on the buy of the century.

If this has ever happened to you you're not alone; in fact, you're in good company to the tune of 90 million other Americans that have that exact same "buzz." It's what's kept QVC (which stands for quality, value and convenience) at the top of the home shopping channel food chain for over 10 years and counting. If you've watched QVC for any length of time (and I highly recommend that you do) you'll notice that while they're serious sellers, there's also a very homey, next-door-neighbor feel to it. It's as though you're sitting with a bunch of friends swapping hot shopping tips, and that's exactly the way QVC wants it. It's what makes their buyers some of the most loyal in the industry. This type of selling "friend to friend" is a relationship builder and while the show may seem folksy, it's anything but. In 2004, QVC racked up $5.7 billion in sales and $760 billion in operating profit making them roughly twice as powerful as Amazon.com; 93 percent of those sales came from repeat customers.

But while QVC might seem like an "anything goes" shopping channel, they take no chances with their products and will quickly remove any item that gets complaints totaling more than one percent of units shipped. Even getting into QVC is tough. On average QVC receives 20,000 applications a year, but only 4 percent of those landed on the show. Why such a low margin? Well first off, QVC knows their audience and so should you. With 90 percent of their product purchased by women this is the primary demographic you'll want to target. Also, keep in mind that as an author you're probably not going to want to tout a book unless it's part of a product line or book series. Independent books don't tend to do well on the show unless you're a celebrity author or the book is a cookbook, which will lend itself to demonstrations. If you're trying to determine whether your book or books are right for QVC their criteria is not that dissimilar from the media. They want something that solves a problem, is easy to demonstrate (so for example if you have an organizing book you could do a messy desk makeover), and is timely. This is what QVC calls "developing your story" and that "story" will end up being your selling tool. When you pitch QVC, they'll want to know right off the bat what your product will do for their viewers, so don't make them guess, point this out right up front in your sales sheet. A full list of product and submission guidelines is available by following the link below. Once you submit your product you'll hear back within three weeks if QVC is interested; if they are, be prepared to put your products through a series of rigorous tests and possible repackaging. Then, QVC will ask you to deliver a minimum of $20,000 in inventory (at wholesale pricing). There is also a series of on-line as well as in-person sessions you'll need to attend before you're "camera ready," but all of this is handled by QVC and segments are often planned at least a month after a product is selected for their show.

Getting a book onto QVC can mean big dollars, in fact books selected have been known to sell as much as $40,000 in product in three and a half minutes of airtime (segments are typically eight minutes in length). The only downside is if you're looking for a spike on a bestseller list, you won't get it through QVC since books sold there do not register in the surveys or databases that contribute to most national best-seller lists. Still a sale is a sale and getting on QVC is a great way to get your book or product out there and make the kind of splash you can only get from a QVC "buzz."

FMI on selling to QVC, head on over to their product submission page: http://www.qvcproductsearch.com/

GETTING INTO CATALOGS

Things are only impossible until they're not.
— *Jean-Luc Picard*

Every year, each of us receives, on average, 78 catalogs and 93 % of us end up ordering from them (I know I do). Each year, over $93 billion in merchandise is sold through the catalog industry. If you have a book that would sell well in a specific catalog, you might want to think seriously about approaching this market. You may have to give them a fairly deep discount. But think of it this way, if you're picked up by a catalog, it could mean moving 1,000 to 40,000 books annually. Sound appealing? Then read on.

It's advisable that you approach these catalog companies as early as possible. Most companies will begin filling a catalog six months prior to mailing. Some companies begin filling them sooner than that. You'll want to contact the individual companies to get their submission forms and find out what their policy is as it relates to Print On Demand. Most catalog companies buy non-returnable, which is perfect for you, but since there are so many different catalogs out there, you'll want to check this first.

Figure out which catalogs would work best with your product, and then submit to them all at once. With your submission package, you should include a well-crafted sales letter along with a handy sales blurb for their catalog. Again, the more work you do for them, the easier you will make their job.

You should plan to follow up on your submission about two weeks after you've mailed it. Do not inquire whether or not they will carry it; just ask them if they got it. It will take about six weeks for them to respond back to you as to whether they will carry it or not. Sometimes they will try your book on a test run (500 to 1000 copies), which is fine. If they do contact you, stay in touch with your publisher, and let them know what's going on. If you do get an initial order, you'll want to make sure to turn it around as quickly as possible. You're going to want to discuss (and possibly negotiate) who gets to pay for shipping. Most of the time the catalog company will pay your shipping costs, but if they don't, you'll want to figure this out before striking a deal. If you get a large order, you may even be able to talk your publisher into footing the bill for shipping. You might also want to discuss this with your publisher prior to submitting your book for consideration. If they are not open to the idea of your book selling through a catalog (hard to believe, I know, but it could happen), then you'll want to know this in advance. This way you can either switch to a publisher who would consider it, or forget about the catalog market altogether.

Depending on the catalog(s) you are targeting, your window of opportunity will vary. Generally, catalog companies will buy during two seasons. For a September catalog, the negotiations need to be completed by the end of July. For a spring catalog, negotiations will need to be completed by December 1. Not all companies adhere to this purchasing window and some even buy their products up to eight times a year.

Got Catalogs?

If you're wondering where to find a list of catalogs, look no further: http://www.catalogs.google.com is a great resource for this! Don't think your book is a match for this market? Scour this site for catalogs using a key word that describes your book and you'll be surprised what you find!

Online Catalog Directories

In order to keep track of the thousands of catalogs published each year, you might want to check out some of the following catalog directories. These online directories are helpful but can, at times, be a bit tedious to navigate. There's a lot of searching involved and you'll end up ordering a ton of catalogs. Fortunately, most of them are free!

Shop at Home Catalogs
www.shopathome.com

The Catalog Shop
http://www.catalogs.com

The Mall of Catalogs
http://www.mallofcatalogs.com

Catalog Link
http://www.cataloglink.com

Major Catalog Companies

Lillian Vernon
Naina Patel, Buyer
445 Hamilton Ave
White Plains, NY 10601
www.lillianvernon.com
(914) 872-2000

According to their buying department, they don't carry many books, but are open to looking at yours if it fits with their catalog. She indicated they don't have specific buying times and are constantly updating their catalogs. Send them a price sheet, a sample of your book, and all other pertinent information mentioned earlier.

Miles Kimball
Becky Kosmeder, Buyer
250 City Center
Oshkosh, WI 54901

Becky is the book buyer for Miles Kimball, and she said that they do not discriminate against self-published authors. As a matter of fact, as long as the book meets the needs of their customers, she's very excited to discover new talent. Submit your book information sheet, the wholesale pricing, a brief book synopsis (if warranted) and an author bio.

The Paragon Catalog
Merchandise
89 Tom Harvey Road
Westerly, RI 02891-0996
http://theparagon.com/

Phone: (401) 596-3000

Paragon emphasizes the finer things in life, but they also offer the quirky, fun, and funny things for office or home. They feature books, and some are partnered with existing products.

Bas Bleu Catalog
Christine Hall, Vice President Marketing
515 Means St. NW
Atlanta, GA 30318-5729
www.basbleu.com
Phone: (404) 577-9462

The Bas Bleu catalog focuses exclusively on books in a variety of categories. Check their Web site to see if your book is a good fit!

CELEBRITY ENDORSEMENTS

A celebrity is a person who works hard all his
life to become well-known, then wears
dark glasses to avoid being recognized.
— Fred Allen

It's a known fact that one complimentary nod from a famous face can launch even the most obscure product. Most advertising agencies pay a high price to have a celebrity take a swig of their soft drink or wear a pair of their running shoes. The good news is, if you can get an endorsement for your book it probably won't cost you a dime; except maybe time, patience, persistence and oh, did I mention patience? It's a long road to get an endorsement, but once traveled it can prove very profitable to the sale of your book.

The first thing you have to remember is that when you're trying to get a celebrity to endorse your book, they're doing you a huge favor. Contact them in the way they wish to be contacted (mail, e-mail or fax) and follow their guidelines (or more than likely, the guidelines their agency dictates) to the letter. Now, your celebrity endorsement might not be from the hottest celebrity. It might a radio personality, a local celebrity, or an author. Who your chosen celebrities are will likely depend on your book. First of all, you're going to want to contact those celebs who have a vested interest in your topic – that will help to greatly increase your chances of getting a response. When you're putting together your list of desired endorsements, start with a long list of people – say 20 or so. One by one, some of these celebs might fall off. "No interest" or "On location" are the two biggest reasons I encounter. So, let's say that the target of your endorsement is an actor, you'll want to start by contacting The Screen Actor's Guild to get their current agent/ publicist information. You can do this by calling (800) 503- 6737 if the celeb you're looking for is LA-based. If they're not, visit www.sag.org for the current contact information for Sag's New York office. If you're trying to reach an author, your best bet will be to head on over to their Web site, determine who their publisher is, and call them. Sometimes the publisher will filter these requests, and sometimes the author has a separate agent who will handle this. Author information can be hard to come by. If you're pursuing someone with obscure contact information, try sending your request to The Author's Guild. If they're a member, The Guild will have their current contact information. You can send an e-mail to staff@authorsregistry. org with your list of names. Once you've gotten contact information for all of your endorsement hopefuls, you'll want to get your package ready to send to them. Some people may want to see a synopsis, outline or press release. Whatever they ask for, make sure it's ready to send off to them right away. The last thing you need is a delay in getting information out to them. You will be requested to mail, e-mail or fax a synopsis and be asked to check back. You'll want to wait a few days to confirm their receipt of this information. At that time, you might get a response "We'll forward this on" or "Sorry, Mr. Such and Such doesn't endorse this type of material." At that point (or later if you're asked to call back), you'll be asked to send your packet.

An endorsement package should include nearly the same information as your review kit: press release, book information, synopsis, and book. With this, you'll also want to include a list of "sample endorsements" much like the mock reviews we discussed earlier in this book. You'll want to have something they can circle and fax or mail back to you. Be sure to include your FedEx envelope or SASE. Your cover letter should be professional and appreciative. Remember, they don't have to do this. It should also indicate that you will forward a copy of the final product once your book is printed and rolling off the presses. Once that package is sent, then it's time to wait and wait and wait and sometimes re-send them a package if they can't seem to locate it. Remember that while this process is long and arduous at times, it's worth every letter, every call and every book mailed out. The truth of the matter is that this is sometimes the least considered marketing aspect of an author's campaign. In fact, most authors I work with never give any thought to celebrity endorsements, even those who have spent years in the business.

A good example of this is an author I have recently had the pleasure of working with. His book, *What I Learned on the Way Down* (Infinity Publishing, 2002), was all about his life as an Emmy award-winning writer, skydiver and personal assistant to Jerry Lewis. The last part stopped me in my tracks. When I asked my client about getting an endorsement from Mr. Lewis he looked at me as though I were speaking Greek. The thought had never occurred to him. In this case, he'd spent so much time with Mr. Lewis he simply never gave it a second thought.

So, when you're figuring out ways to market your book, give some consideration to celebrity endorsements. You might even know someone who knows someone who knows someone, narrowing those six degrees of separation. If you don't, then you'll have to go about it the old fashioned way. In either case, getting even one famous face to acknowledge your work is often enough to get the most apprehensive buyer to give your book a second look. And in the end, isn't that what it's all about?

If you're trying to track down that celebrity to garner an endorsement, here is a resource for you:

www.celebrity-addresses.com. You can try this site out for a fee of $4.95 for a three-day trial, after that it's $14.95 a month.

SPIN-OFF PRODUCTS: CREATING MORE SALES OPTIONS FOR YOUR BOOK

I'm all in favor of keeping dangerous weapons out of the hands of fools. Let's start with typewriters.
— *Frank Lloyd Wright*

You don't have to be "Cheers" to create a successful spin-off. In fact, more and more authors are creating products based on their book. If you feel you've exhausted all the potential sales options for your book, and even if you haven't, spin-offs might be an area you should consider. So, what exactly are spin-offs? Well, they can be anything really, as long as it is related to your book. Spin-offs can be actual products like screensavers, mouse pads, stuffed toys, but possibly more practical and less complicated. Spin-offs can also be special reports, audio products, booklets, and tip sheets. Most of these are easy to create and even easier to promote, especially if you have a book that offers itself up to being sectioned out into individual informational pieces.

The first of these products we'll talk about are audio products. Either in compact disc or audio tape, audio products can really enhance your bottom line. These audio offers can be portions of your book, they can be the book itself, or they can be a separate and entirely new offering, perhaps a continuation of your book's topic. If you do any teaching or lecturing, you can often tape these sessions and offer them later as an individual product. Take them to a local audio/visual studio and have them remastered, duplicated, and labeled. Now, you've got something to add to your Web site.

Booklets can be another way to enhance your repertoire of offerings. Paulette Ensign has made a business of tip booklets, both having her own library of booklets and teaching others how to create them. Her Web site, www.tipsbooklets.com, is packed with information and products to help any author get started. "A single manuscript of a tips booklet can be recycled over and over again," says Paulette, "and you can develop a new income stream with each and every deal. The booklet can be created from a book you've already written, a newsletter that is part of your ongoing world, or from sound bites you continually share with clients, audiences or anyone who will listen." Booklets can be sold individually, they can be customized for clients or organizations and they can often be a very inexpensive way to get in the door of a potential organization that might not otherwise be available to you. Let's say for example you want to offer your book as a subscriber incentive to a magazine. Typically magazines won't have the budget to offer something quite as expensive as a book to their new subscribers. Although it does happen, it's much easier if you can offer them something that only costs them pennies, but leverages them a big return. Booklets can accomplish this.

I love special reports and so do my customers. My Web site is packed with them. In fact, I am continually updating content on my site to include new and exciting reports for new and returning customers. Special reports can be anything. They can be an excerpted part of your book, new chapters you weren't able to include, updated information on your topic. They can even be templates or worksheets. The possibilities are endless. Take a look at my special reports page: http://amarketingexpert. com/store/. We've got a myriad of reports to chose from, all excerpted from *Get Published Today*. Better still, while it takes six to nine months to publish a fully updated version of *Get Published Today*, it takes only hours to update and reload these reports, giving our customers freshly updated content on a regular basis.

Tip sheets can be another way to add to your bottom line. Recently, I was in the midst of a special sales deal with a company for a book we were working on. The company loved the book, but couldn't afford to purchase it. Since they were already "sold" on the book, I knew I had an in with them. I suggested that we offer them a tip sheet. This would be given free to their customers, thereby allowing them to benefit from the book they loved so much. This process gave the company the ability to share the vital information gleaned from the book, without it costing them a dime. My client excerpted portions of his book, fashioning them into informative tip sheets and offering them to this company. They then printed them off, adding their logo and passed them out to their new customers. They estimated that they would pass out around a half a million tip sheets a quarter. There are few authors I know that can afford this type of advertising.

When you're tinkering with your marketing plan, make sure to include spin-off products whenever possible. Whether big or small, paid or freebie, they are what I call the Bread Crumbs

Factor. In the end it all leads back to you and your book, and isn't that what you want your marketing plan to do?

SECTION FIVE

THE MEDIA

Never judge a book by its movie.

— J.W. Eagan

CRACKING THE CODE

*Consider the postage stamp. It secures success through
its ability to stick to one thing until it gets there.*
— *Josh Billings*

Getting into the media spotlight may seem at times like cracking some secret code. It's not easy, I'll grant you that, and it does require persistence the likes of which you've never seen. It takes a passion for your work, a sunny disposition when you hear "no," and a lion's share of courage to keep pressing on when no one seems to care that you've written a novel destined to be a classic. I hope the information in the next several pages helps to shed a bit of light on the elusive and all too intriguing media frenzy. But don't stop there. I've only scratched the surface in this book as far as national media contacts go. There are many, many more places for you to look. Take your focus off of the national spotlight and look around your own back yard. You probably have a local talk show, morning show or radio program (or two) you can try to sway with your outstanding media kit and story idea. And that's the trick. Come up with a be-all and end-all story idea, believe in what you're doing and pitch until you have knocked on every door imaginable.

The Secret to Finding Freelancers

So let's say you've got a great story idea and can't seem to get through to the major media targets, what do you do? Well how about searching for freelancers! How? Well it's easy. Just type in "freelancer" or "freelancer writer" and the topic or print publication name (if you're looking for freelancers who are tied to specific magazines or newspapers). Most freelancers have Web sites which you can peruse along with their contact info; some will even have tips for pitching them stories.

PITCHING YOUR STORY IDEA

*Be shameless. Try anything within
reason to get your book noticed.*
— *William Targ*

Okay, so you've got a great book-related story idea. Now what? Well, now it's time to begin knocking on some doors. It's time to start pitching that idea. But where and how do you begin? First, study your intended target. Watch their show. Listen to their station. Read their magazine or newspaper. Knowing who you're pitching to is half your battle. When you're doing this research, ask yourself what the demographic is of the viewer, listener, or reader. This will save you the cost of sending a book to someone who might not be interested. You'll also save the person at the other end the time of having to read through your material and toss your stuff in their circular file.

Those Tricky E-Mail Subject Lines

We all know how important e-mail subject lines are when you're pitching the media but are there any tricks to getting noticed? You bet. Try this. And I mean quite literally "this" - this is a powerful word and when used correctly can help entice reporters to open your e-mail. Another powerful word is "here" as in "Here's the answer" and also, try using an ellipsis (...), they create what has been referred to as "brain itch" forcing the reader to, well, read on ...

There's also an art to pitching effectively. First of all, when you're pitching a television show (and sometimes radio too), pitch a segment. In other words your pitch packet (or e-mail) should be a segment suggestion as opposed to a simple pitch. When pitching a segment, you'll want to keep in mind that television is a visual medium. Now, while this may sound obvious to some, you'll be surprised at how many people still pitch a dry segment. In other words, they'll suggest a segment on themselves and their book with no footage or additional guests. Shows (especially morning shows and night time programs like Dateline) don't want talking heads. They're boring and they don't keep the audience's attention. You want to catch those channel surfers and get them to stop surfing and start watching. They'll take on average a second or two to decide if they want to stick around. Keep them enthralled and you've managed to capture the toughest audience. Also, when you're pitching, forget about pitching yourself. Pitch issues instead, pitch something newsworthy or controversial. If you can, try to tie your book into a news angle or a recent headline. Pitching issues is a great way to get noticed. For example, if your book is on obsessive behavior (i.e. stalking), suggest a topic that would entice them. For example, "Obsession isn't flattery." Then suggest one or two guest speakers who might bring up a controversial side of this topic. If you can package it like this, you've just helped a producer create a show and made their job easier. Remember to pitch your area of expertise, whatever you've determined that to be. Now find out what your angle is and build from there. If that angle doesn't seem to be working then create a new one. The thing is to keep trying.

E-mail seems to be growing as the preferred method of pitching these days. In a recent survey conducted by Bacon's Media Guide, an overwhelming 70% of editors indicated their pitching preference was e-mail followed by mail, fax, and the phone.

Check out the following stats:

E-mail 70%

U.S. Mail 14%

FAX 11%

Phone 5%

The figures above really help show the levels by which e-mail pitching has grown in the last few years. For many of us e-mail pitching is an easy, effective, and inexpensive way for us to promote. The downside to this is that many e-mail pitches have become a form of SPAM, especially in recent years with the proliferation of e-mail viruses and permission marketing. Many reporters get upwards of 300 legitimate e-mails a day, some even get as many as 1,000. This figure does not include unwanted e-mails or SPAM. With that many e-mails filling their mailbox, one sure way to get on a reporter's nerves is to send a pitch that is too long, incomplete, and untargeted. It's a fine line between e-mail pitches and spamming.

Recently, an author friend of mine told me he submitted a story idea to several media outlets via e-mail. And, he pitched them all at once. This means that with one click of the mouse, you can save yourself hours of faxing time, hundreds of sheets of paper and get your message out across the country, right? Wrong. Editors, reporters and news people really don't like it when you mass e-mail them. It's inconsiderate and it's annoying and it's a surefire way to get your story ignored. If you're going to pitch by e-mail and you've confirmed it with the source that they prefer an initial contact made via e-mail, then go for it. But don't mass e-mail.

Because of the extensive e-mail pitches reporters are receiving, some have begun investing in e-mail services to help them filter out unwanted mail. To avoid getting your pitch sent to the delete bin, there are a few things you can do to help position your pitch for better consideration.

- First, make sure you're pitching the correct person for your story. If you're not, don't ask them to forward it on to the right person. When in doubt, check their Web site or call to find out where to send your pitch.

- Always put your news hook in the subject line. A news hook should be no more than three to five words. Also, include the name of your author, company, or book title beside your news hook so a busy reporter can quickly identify your e-mail. Don't send an e-mail that has this in the subject line: "News release from XYZ" and make

them search through the e-mail to find your news hook.
Remember, it's an e-mail pitch not a scavenger hunt.

- Always use the "above the fold" rule. This means that
  you make sure your pitch appears above the fold in any e-
  mailed (or faxed) release. Ideally, your news hook should
  appear in the subject line of your e-mail and then again
  in the first few lines of the release. If your subject line
  is a "teaser" then the teaser should be explained in the
  first few lines of your pitch. By teaser I mean a line that
  will help pique the reporter's interest. Usually a teaser
  line is in the form of a question. The answer to whatever
  question you used should then be aptly explained in the
  first few lines of the pitch.

- Don't send attachments! This is probably one of the biggest
  pet peeves of any reporter or producer. Not just because
  of viruses, but because it's an additional step they have to
  take to open your pitch. Build a pressroom on your Web
  site. More and more, the media is going electronic and
  so should your media kit. Put the entire contents of your
  media kit on your Web site and let the media peruse your
  bio, press releases, and book information right there on
  the Web. Even if you pitch them electronically you can
  still include a short sentence to direct them to your site.
  For example: "For a complete media kit, please visit:
  www.yourWeb site.com." But always offer to send them
  one in case they don't want to view it electronically.

- Don't forget your contact information. I can't tell you
  how many producers I've spoken with who tell me this is
  the first thing people forget. Don't assume that a reporter
  will reply to your e-mail. They may need to pick up the

phone for a more immediate response. If your number isn't included, guess what? Neither is your story. The moral of this story? Don't just point and click your way through a campaign. Instead, pretend that on each e-mail, you will be required to affix a 37-cent stamp. This alone will prevent you from sending a press release about your book signing in Milwaukee to an editor in San Diego.

Want to seem like an old pro at TV lingo? Here are a few terms you'll need to know:

B-roll: secondary footage, usually played in the background during an interview

Sound byte: a short 7-12 second blurb

VO: voice over

Package: a 1 to 2 min segment on your topic

Timing Your Pitch

When you pitch is almost as important as what you pitch. Before you start calling that editor or producer, turn on you radio or television to make sure there isn't a breaking story happening the day you want to pitch your topic. I had a producer tell me once that she got a call for a pitch on the day JFK, Jr.'s plane went down. "I couldn't have been less interested or more eager to get off the phone," she said.

Sometimes the best times to pitch are when government offices are closed. If the government isn't making news, reporters are often scrambling to find a story to cover. Go through your calendar and start circling government holidays; then get ready to pitch!

Besides being aware of other significant stories, you'll also want to be aware of other things that can help your pitch. First, you'll want to see what you can hang your star on. In other words, what else is going on in the media that can tie into your story? You'll want to find your angle, something that is already top of mind that you can comment on or offer an alternative perspective. Start scanning the news and newspapers, see what's going on around the country that your book might tie into. If you're looking for local coverage as opposed to national exposure, then maybe you want to give a national story a local angle. Either way, you'll need to have some sort of tie-in to make this work.

Besides ongoing news stories, other tie-ins might include: celebrities, upcoming movie releases or current blockbusters, weather, and holidays. To give you an example of using the movie angle, when *A Beautiful Mind* came out I was promoting a book on male depression. What better tie-in than an author who could comment on the character Russell Crowe was portraying and how he suffered with depression for years. When Brad Pitt and Jennifer Aniston broke up, another author of mine was promoting his book on how to maintain a healthy relationship; what better time to offer his comment than when the world was buzzing about 'Brangelina'?

Besides being aware of current trends or news items in the media, you'll also want to be aware of seasonal topics. These are called the seasons of publicity and no matter what else is going on, one or all of these topics will find their way into a news story. Here's a look at news topics by quarter:

January – April

The media is looking to the future, trend spotting stories are big, as are yearly predications, dieting stories, and how to keep your finances in order (this will especially tie into any story you pitch in April). There will also be a lot of talk of organizing and quitting smoking as well as anything and everything to do with New Year's resolutions and spring cleaning.

May – August

As we approach the May-June timeframe, many stories will start to turn from spring fever, to summer vacations, things to do with your kids, and so on. The summer months are a great time to get publicity because so many people go on vacation and reporters are often scrambling for stories. You can pitch a lot of your fun, fluff angles, book releases, fun reads, things to do and don't forget the all important stories surrounding Memorial Day and Fourth of July.

September – December

During this timeframe, the media's attention starts to turn to back-to-school and education-themed stories. We're also inching towards a very busy time of year during which the media begins to focus on end of the year stories, holiday ideas and "taking stock" topics recapping the prior 12 months. December is a great time to pitch your fluff pieces as many newsrooms are operating on skeleton crews. Quirky and fun stories are perfect to pitch around the holidays as are relationship and diet topics (getting along with your family, losing weight in the New Year).

If you don't think you can offer advice on a particular topic, think again. Just like becoming an expert, you're there to offer commentary and feedback whenever you can. If something is happening in the news that ties into your topic somehow, but you have a different viewpoint, craft a press release and send it off; the media loves differing viewpoints especially if they offer a controversial angle. No controversy? No problem. Soft and fuzzy sells well too. Just watch your local news during the last few minutes of programming and you'll see that they regularly use the softer pieces they like to call "fluff" or kickers. Kickers are the short, up pieces most news programs like to end with. It leaves the viewer feeling good at the end of what might have been a pretty depressing broadcast.

Trying to tie your book into an upcoming movie release? Here are a few databases that will help you do just that:

http://upcomingmovies.com

http://movies.searchwho.com

Both of these sites offer extensive databases on upcoming releases of movies and DVD's

Marketing Tip

Get a copy of the editorial calendar for a newspaper or magazine you're trying to pitch. This is a listing of special sections and topics they have planned throughout the year.

Review the calendar and find a specific issue where your topic would be a good fit. Then, call the publication, ask for the name of the person who edits that section and write or e-mail them with your story idea. Try to do this several months in advance and keep in mind that the larger the magazine, the longer their lead times or the sooner they will "close" an issue. Some magazines close issues as far ahead as six months in advance! Here's a general guideline of when magazines close their issues:

Trade publications: two to four months

Regional magazines: two to four months

National magazines: six to eight months

Cost Savings Tip

Pitching a magazine or newspaper can be a costly endeavor, especially if you are targeting several different publications. Also, you might "think" a magazine or newspaper is right for your market, then after subscribing, you find that it isn't. One way of not having to empty your pocketbook at a newsstand or ending up with 20 different subscriptions is to frequent your local library to see what issues they carry. Spend an afternoon researching your publication. If that's not an option for you, there are a number of magazine sites that offer free trial issues when you sign up. That way, you can get a look at the magazine and decide whether it's the right publication for your work before you spend the money subscribing. Remember, if you do end up subscribing, keep a note of it for your yearly taxes. Subscriptions are the first thing people forget to write off because they usually aren't accompanied by a receipt.

The Celebrity Craze (how to make the most of it)

Do you have a book or story that has a celebrity tie- in and could be pitched to a celebrity-driven magazine? If you haven't considered this you might want to.

According to the Audit Bureau of Circulation, newsstand circulation for celebrity-driven mags rose significantly in the first half of 2005 (driven by the numerous scandals and hot stories a la Brad, Jennifer, Angelina, Katie and Tom). People Magazine, for example, saw its circulation jump from 1.3% to 3.8 million. US Weekly rose 24% to a total circulation of 1.67 million, Star Magazine jumped 21% to 1.42 million and In Touch grew an astounding 50% to 1.12 million. Just this week OK Magazine, a UK publication, launched their first issue in the US.

We're a celebrity crazed nation -- even Oprah, the "grand dame" of spirituality, has been featuring more celebs on her show so if you're not playing the celebrity angle you might want to, it could be a star- studded media extravaganza.

Following Up

When it comes to pitching your stuff, tenacity should be your middle name. I encourage you to keep following up on your pitch until you get a "no." And even then, wait an appropriate length of time, maybe a few months, and then try pitching again. If you get a comment like: "it's wrong for our format," move on, but if the response is "not right now, but maybe in the future," that's your key to stay in touch. Wait about seven to 10 days to start making follow-up calls; more for bigger media targets.

If you actually get to talk to the person you're pitching and don't land up in voice mail, you might think about starting your conversation with: "Is this a good time?" or "Are you on a deadline?" This shows that you understand that they are busy. You are respectful of their time and you're beginning to win them over. Next, be concise in your statement, whether you're speaking to someone live or on voice mail. A trick I learned years ago was to smile when you talk. It's a good thing to remember because your smile comes across on the telephone.

Whatever you do, don't let any sense of impatience you might feel bleed through to your conversation. The person on the other end will pick up on that. It must sound like you're calling them for the first time, not the hundredth. And remember as you're pushing through your follow-up pitch list: what doesn't interest the media today, might interest them tomorrow or maybe even next year. Stay in front of them; keep sending newsworthy, relevant press releases. Send your postcards... whatever it takes. Be persistent but don't be obnoxious. Jenice Gharib, editor of *Vision Magazine*, suggests that following up should be an art rather than a science. "I think it is really important to develop an ongoing relationship with an editor," she says. "Prior to your book release and after it." Especially with local magazines, papers, or trade journals. Editors are more inclined to review or write about books and authors they know. That doesn't mean the 'out of the blue' book won't get in. It just gives them a better chance.

The Sounds of Silence

If your media campaign has come to a grinding halt check your calendar, it might be August. August is a notoriously quiet time of year. Why? Well, historically it's been *the* month for the media to take vacations and for New York to go "dark."

Your Pitching Script

I've never written a script when I call the media. I think it sounds too canned. What I do, however, is make up a list of points or highlights I want to make sure to mention. Also, it's important for me to know exactly why I'm calling. Or what I wish to accomplish with my call. If you do get someone on the phone and don't end up in voice mail, knowing what your purpose is will help direct the call exactly where you want it to go. When you're determining this, be specific. Finally, if you don't sound crisp and directed, the person on the other end will become disinterested very quickly.

Happy Holidays; Leveraging the Holidays to Your Advantage

Did you know that some of the best pitching is done during the holidays? Why? Because while the world gets caught up in the season, the news shows must go on. Newsrooms tend to operate with skeleton crews as reporters and producers take the last of their vacation days. Pitches slow to a crawl during a time when reporters really need them.

Here are tactics you can use to get the most mileage from your pitch and help, not hinder, the media during this festive time.

1. Pitch the wire services

Regional dailies really depend on wire stories to get them through the holiday crunch. The media will often rely more heavily on wire services because of shorter workdays and limited staff.

2. Repitch your rejects

The holidays are a great time to re-pitch stories that were rejected earlier in the year. Why? Well, maybe it didn't get rejected for content, but because a more significant story took precedence at that time. The holiday slow-down is a great time to repackage and repitch that story.

3. Don't hesitate to pitch at the last minute

You'd be surprised to find out how many people are "no shows" for radio interviews or how many stations wait until the last minute to fill an interview slot. If you've got a great New Year's resolution story, pitch it just before Christmas or during the Christmas/New Year shut down.

Making Your Holiday Cards a Cool PR Tool

When you mail your holiday cards, don't forget to thank the manager at the bookstore where you did a signing. Or maybe you should thank the reporter who interviewed you. Taking a moment to send a greeting and "thank you" goes a long way in our electronic society. It's also a great way to keep your name (and your book) in front of them. So make a list of anyone who helped promote your book and send a quick holiday greeting to them all, thanking thank them for their contribution to your book's success. They'll remember you the next time you call!

Media Gifts – What's Appropriate and What's Not

And speaking of holidays...it's perfectly OK to say "thank you" with more than a holiday greeting, just make sure you're not overstepping professional boundaries. Journalists typically shy away from accepting anything, but can, technically, accept gifts under $25. The rules change somewhat when it comes to TV. Simply put: they love food. If you want to say "thank you" to a local TV station, send them food. Extravagant, over-the-top gifts are never appropriate and might be construed as bribery, so don't send a case of champagne or rack of lamb! In fact, if you're going to do a gift, do something that ties into your book or topic!

I Spy

Google has a great service called Google Alerts: http://google.com/alerts. If you're trying to keep tabs on how many media mentions you're getting, what's being said about your topic or trying to keep an eye on the competition then this service is for you. It's free and very accurate; we use it all the time!

SEVEN MEDIA MYTHS THAT WILL KILL YOUR CAMPAIGN!

If there's a book you really want to read, but it hasn't been written yet, then you must write it.

— *Toni Morrison*

When it comes to media sometimes it's hard to know what to believe and what to dismiss. The truth is that you'll be told a lot of stories when it comes to pitching, not all of them are true. Here are some myths to avoid.

Myth #1: A good news release is all you need to get "ink"

The days of the "one size fits all" news releases are gone. Now it's all about customizing and knowing what the media target you're pitching is looking for. Making one release isn't a bad idea, but use it as a starting point, not the final message.

Myth #2: Mention your book every chance you get

The surest way to kill an interview (and your chances of getting asked back) is when you mention your book over and over. When you say things like: "as I wrote in my book" you'll cheapen your message and make it look too sales-like. Viewers hate being sold, give them solid information and they'll buy your book because they'll want to know more.

Myth #3: You must answer every question the media asks you

Despite all your research and expertise, you can't expect to know everything. If you don't know an answer don't lie or speculate. It's much better to say: "You know I don't know the answer to that question, but I'm happy to look into it and get back to you," than to make up a story that will make you (and the reporter) look bad.

Myth #4: You can use advertising dollars to influence media interviews

If you're trying to get some airtime or print placement, do not ever allude to buying ad space in order to get them to commit to an interview. This is a completely unethical thing to do, conversely, if someone is trying to get you to buy an ad in order to be considered for their publication or program, run for the hills.

Myth #5: Use big, complicated words; they'll make you sound savvy

It's unfortunate, but the "dumbing down of America" is a necessary trend and one you shouldn't overlook. Do not use complicated industry jargon to impress your audience (unless you're speaking to industry experts), you will only confuse them and alienate the person interviewing you.

Myth #6: Emotion is a bad thing

Marketing fact: People buy on emotion. Whether it's happy, sad, or angry. Make them feel something and you'll send them straight to your Web site to buy your book. Now I'm not suggesting that you fall apart on camera, but emotion is a good thing. Look human! If it's a subject that you're passionate about, look passionate! If it's a terrible thing you went through that you're writing about, let your audience "feel" that emotion right along with you!

Myth #7: You should never even consider doing an interview without media training

Don't get me wrong, media training is a great thing, but media training without the proper interview prep work can lead to a disaster. For example, don't assume because you're media trained that you can survive any interview without researching the show or publication. Even worse, don't put all your focus on your media training and then forget to update your data to support your interview.

Keeping Tabs on your Book

Junglescan.com is a great way to keep tabs on how your book is going on sites like Aamzon.com and BN.com. Just input your ISBN and watch the system do its thing. You can monitor this over days, weeks, or months. There's no limit for tracking and no limit to how many books you can track!

CRAFTING YOUR ELEVATOR PITCH

There is no elevator to success. You have to take the stairs.
— Unknown

Imagine this: You're in the elevator with the producer of your favorite show. The program you've been trying to get on for years. What would you say to this person? Would you comment on the weather? Perhaps lament about the price of gas? Or would you take the opportunity to pitch your story as you glide up three floors? Now, this might not actually ever happen, but it's still a good idea to be prepared. That's what I call your elevator pitch.

So, how do you get to your elevator pitch? How do you refine your topic down in such a way that it grabs the attention of someone in a matter of a few seconds? Getting to the heart of your story is the first part to this. The "heart" of your story is what everything else is built around. I taught a class once on writer focus; the single objective of this class was to pare down a story until it was so refined, and so focused that a 250-page book could be described in one minute. To some, this type of manuscript refinement might seem unrealistic and counterintuitive to everything they've ever learned about writing. But whether you are querying literary agents or trying to get into the media, you'll need to know your elevator pitch.

To get an idea of some great elevator pitches, go to the movies and watch the trailers for upcoming projects. Movie trailers are a great way to learn about elevator pitches. In a matter of 30 seconds, a movie producer has broken down every aspect of his or her movie in a few clear, concise messages. Enough to get you interested in seeing their forthcoming movie. That's the essence of an elevator pitch. Breaking your story down into a clear, concise statement (or few sentences) to pique the interest of your target media, reviewer, or reader.

So... how do you get to your elevator pitch? Start by focusing on the core of your book. What's the one thread that carries through your manuscript, the one topic or story that everything else circles around? If your response to that is: "Well, there are actually five things that go on in this book." I'd say that's fine, but keep in mind that without that one thing, the rest of the book wouldn't exist. Another way to get to this "core" is to ask yourself (or have someone help you with this) "what are the benefits to the reader" or "what will my reader learn?" That is the answer to your question. That is the core of your book.

Again, your reader will probably walk away from your tome with many other benefits, but there is one that is paramount over all others. That's your focus, that's what your book is about. So let creativity and your muse be your guide but always remember to focus, focus, focus!

WHEN OLD NEWS
IS GOOD NEWS

Writing is a dog's life, but the only life worth living.
— Gustave Flaubert

Sometimes when you're pitching your topic or learning the art of the media pitch all you will hear is "your topic must be newsworthy, it must be trendy and it must tie into a current/relevant topic." So let's say you have a great pitch, the only thing is it's from last year. Is old news good news? Sometimes, yes it is. If your pitch ties into something current and relevant then it's what we call an "evergreen." In fact, I have pitches that I've used several times over, they are seasonal pitches that become relevant when that particular season rolls around. Let me give you an example.

Let's say you have a book on relationships and Valentine's Day is looming on the horizon. Well, you might create a pitch or two for this holiday and strike media gold when it comes to their interest in your topic. But once the holiday is history you can still file away your pitch, providing it wasn't pivotal to a news-topic that won't be coming around again.

Several years ago I created a topic for Valentine's Day called: "The one thing people DON'T do that screws up their marriages." Now since divorce rates aren't getting any better for the foreseeable future, this topic will continue to remain fresh year after year. Certainly I might tweak a sentence or two or offer a fresh set of tips or questions, but the pitch itself remains consistent.

So, how do you go about creating evergreen hooks for your book? Well, start this as you would any campaign and open a calendar to map out the next 12 months of your marketing efforts. During those 12 months you will no doubt find a pitch or two that you can recycle the next time this date comes around. Or, alternatively, you might find a topic that isn't date sensitive, meaning that it can be used over and over again with a few minor changes. Health, relationship, and diet issues all tend to have this "evergreen" component to them. We're equally interested in this topic no matter what the season, so for example, when the holidays come around people are talking about family issues, dieting issues, etc. And while they might have a different twist to them, the pitch is essentially the same. This also holds true for a book you are promoting year after year. Let's say you have a health book, and while you keep updating the book with current trends and related information the content is essentially the same. Save for a few references to the low-carb craze your pitches might be quite similar year after year. Or better still, a book on personal finance or relationships. These are the staples of our lives and barring any new research, remain fairly static throughout our lives.

Creating evergreens for your topic will allow you the freedom and flexibility you need to keep the momentum going on your campaign without siphoning off an overwhelming amount of creativity every time an appropriate seasonal angle comes along. Knowing when to craft a fresh release and when to recycle an old one will go a long way to keeping your media campaign strong and perhaps a tad less time-consuming.

Wedding Bells

Do you have a topic that can be geared to the bridal market? If you haven't considered pitching this area perhaps you should. Bridal magazines typically have a readership turnover every six to 14 months and there are certain topics (wedding planning, food, flowers, dieting, etc.) that are repeated in every issue. While all magazines are clamoring for that creative edge, bridal magazines have to be especially careful since it's necessary to keep a fresh angle on topics featured in every issue. Also, consider this: bridal magazines have the longest shelf life since most bridal salons, caterers, etc. keep slews of back issues for reference, gown selection, etc. (your local doctor's office with outdated magazines had nothing on this market). This means, of course, a potential for increased exposure. So the next time you're getting creative with your pitch ask yourself how you might angle to this market.

Happy Wedding!

ARE YOU READY WHEN THE MEDIA CALLS?

Sex on television can't hurt you unless you fall off.
— *Author Unknown*

Are you prepared for the media to call you? If you're not, you should be. Pitching is great, but if you're not ready when the call finally comes in, it is really just a wasted effort. Most authors go about their routine of sending press releases, e-mailing pitches or mailing books, but they're unprepared for the caller that says, "Yes, I'd like to interview you for a story I'm doing." Most likely the interviewer is calling several people; being prepared will give you a leg up on the competition.

As thorough as you're being in your pitch to them, you'll need to be equally thorough when they call you. The first step is to keep a file close at hand with a list of places you've pitched and the angle you've given them. Most reporters won't take the time to reconfirm the slant you took or the ideas you offered; having this handy will give the impression of someone who is on top of their media campaign. Taking the time to dig or reconstruct this information is unprofessional and will reflect badly on you.

Next, have all your tip sheets handy. If you didn't submit tips to the media in your pitch (and even if you did), you'll

175

want to offer these to the person interviewing you. It's also important to keep up with current events that might add a new twist to your topic. When relevant to your industry, it's also a good idea to stay up to date with new research that might shed some additional light on your subject matter. Also, keep a list of other experts in your field to help the reporter or producer flesh out a story. If you do your homework, they won't need to call anyone else, but in case they do, have this information handy, especially if they can offer a different perspective than yours. Remember, it's the media's job to offer all sides of the story. Keep in mind that this is not just about getting them the information they need, but also ingratiating yourself to the media and becoming their No. 1 contact for this particular topic. Be generous. The more you can help them do their job, the better an interview will go, and the chances are very likely you'll get called on again.

Be courteous of their time and be aware of their deadlines. If they need to see a copy of your book and they're local, offer to drop it off. If they aren't local, do whatever you can to get the book to them on time, even if this means incurring overnight mailing fees. The more you can help them enhance their segment or print piece, the more time or "ink" you might get. Also, if there are pictures or digital files related to your subject matter, make sure you have them handy and can e-mail them with a few clicks of a mouse. It's tedious and time-consuming to have to scan these first (or have them scanned) before they are in a format that can be quickly transferred from interviewee to the reporter.

I tested these ideas a couple of years ago when the San Diego Union-Tribune contacted me to ask me one question about my topic. Because I had everything ready and was able to update them on new developments, this one question turned into a front-page story. When it comes to the media, be a Boy Scout: Be prepared, or be prepared to give up a story to someone who is.

Face Time

Are you itching to get face-time with some of your local media? How about joining one of your local press clubs? Virtually every city has them. Try searching your local club on Google by typing in "press club and your city." Then see when their next meeting is.

FATAL PR: MISTAKES AUTHORS MAKE ON THEIR CAMPAIGNS

Experience is the name every one gives to their mistakes.
— *Oscar Wilde*

Any author who is driving his or her own PR campaign knows that often times marketing and media can be an uphill battle. Many times authors are pitching and promoting themselves with minimal results. It can be tedious and frustrating and sometimes leads them to make fatal PR mistakes that can cost them their campaign.

One of the first, and potentially most fatal mistakes, is thinking that one or two media appearances are going to wing your book into the bestseller spotlight. Media works when it's done consistently and often it takes months, and in some cases years, for you to reach your own "PR payoff." The most important part of a campaign is the author's ability to stick with it. Most of the interviews you see nationally, on shows like Good Morning America and Oprah, started with a regional buzz. Build your base (or buzz) in your own back yard first and then start getting your message out on a national level. And this leads us to our second PR mistake: ignoring regional or trade media. Sometimes when you're promoting yourself it's easy to get caught up in going after the big fish, but don't ignore the smaller regional and niche publications, they can be a gold mine of PR and really help to get the buzz going.

Next on our list of fatal PR mistakes is the technique with which authors pitch themselves. First and foremost you want to make sure you're pitching the right people, don't just go after a "producer," find the producer that's right for the story. And be cautious of when you pitch, before you start calling the media, turn on your TV or radio and see if there's a breaking news story. There's no quicker way to offend your media target than by pitching them a story when they're scrambling to cover a plane crash or some other major disaster.

As you're navigating through your PR campaign you'll also want to make sure your pitches are focused and relevant. It's much easier to get the attention of the media when you're pitching them something that's already on their radar screen. For example, remember when you're putting together your campaign to keep an eye out for seasonal or news spins to your topic. If, let's say, you are discussing the topic of depression, you might want to pitch it around a nationally designated "depression awareness day" or, perhaps, given all the buzz around college kids and depression, you might want to tackle this as a back-to-school issue. Targeted, focused pitches are the best way to get the media to notice you, so open that calendar or read your local newspaper to find out what's hot and top of mind. Also, respect their time when you're pitching. Get to the point, don't ramble and remember that this is not about you, it's about the benefits to their readers, viewers, or listeners and most of all, never, ever, ever sell your book. You should always sell yourself and your expertise. Producers and editors will be looking for the WIIFM factor behind your pitch (what's in it for me) not how they can showcase your book.

Finally there's no quicker way to end your campaign than to over promise, stretch the truth, or not be reliable. If you miss an interview or over promise on a commitment one time, you can kiss any further media goodbye. Word travels fast in the industry and bad news travels even faster. Remember: be patient, be persistent, and be professional and you're bound to get the media you deserve and keep your campaign alive and well!

Getting to Newspapers

Yahoo has just about every imaginable newspaper and you can peruse them all here: http://dir.yahoo.com/news_and_media/newspapers/

C-SPAN

Don't be afraid to take a big step.
You can't cross a chasm in two small jumps.
— David Lloyd George

C-Span offers a myriad of good programs you should consider pitching. Specifically, *BookTV* is a great avenue for authors to get out information on their books. Since its inception, C-Span's BookTV has covered topics from children's books to history books, political novels to social issues. They also focus on events around the world, live signings, author interviews and publishing world updates. Their programs are cutting edge and very well put together. BookTV has proven to be a great instrument for authors, and they welcome ideas, suggestions and innovative ways authors are making a difference in the literary world.

To submit a program idea to BookTV, contact:

Amy Roach, Producer or
Andrew Murray, Producer
C-Span2
400 North Capital Street NW, Suite 650
Washington, DC 20001
Phone: (202) 737-3220
Fax: (202) 737-0580

E-mail: aroach@c-span.org
E-mail: amurray@c-span.org

Mail a press kit, or contact the producers directly via telephone. If they're interested, they'll contact you. Amy's particular areas of interest are politics and current affairs. Andrew likes to see anything involving history and biography.

THE MORNING SHOWS

Whoever controls the media controls the culture.
— *Allen Ginsberg*

Every author has at some point nurtured the dream of getting on a high-profile morning show. How someone goes about doing this is a whole different matter. The pressure is really on for producers to find stories that are gripping and visual and not too complicated. Keep it simple and keep it interesting. That's the bottom line. And remember that if you're featured on one show, you probably won't be featured on another. Unless you're the hottest story in the country, most morning shows won't follow their competitors. This does not mean that you can't pitch all three shows at once, you'll just need to mention it in your cover letter. Let them know that you're pitching other shows, that way they know you'll probably go with whoever gets to you first.

If you're going for national television it will be crucial for you to have prior media exposure. Most of the national shows won't feature someone who is "green," meaning that the intended guest hasn't had any type of televised media experience. It's also an added bonus if you've been properly media trained. That way they know they are getting someone who not only has the experience but also has spent the time it takes to learn the various components to a successful interview.

Here's another little-known secret: if you aspire to be on national media, try focusing on creating a regional buzz about your book. Many of the producers of these shows scour local papers to find the stories buried on page five that are destined to be tomorrow's headliners. In fact, the executive producer at *The Today Show* reads 35 regional papers a day. Many times that's where they find their stories: the stories no one else is covering yet, and that's what they want. A story that's new, fresh and something no one else has featured.

The Art of the Morning Show Pitch

Pitching any show is truly an art form, but morning shows are a league unto themselves. Most authors don't realize this until they are knee-deep in their own marketing campaign. The art of the pitch is a quite serious matter to any producer fielding stories from would-be television guests. And one of the first things they will tell you is to first off, watch their show. Now, while that may seem like an obvious thing to do, most authors who pitch themselves don't really know the demographics of the show they're targeting. For example, if you're pitching something to a national morning show (i.e. *The Today Show*, *Good Morning America*, *The Early Show*), you'll need to know that the attention span of anyone watching is about 20 minutes. With individual segments running about seven minutes each, it's rare for a viewer to watch a morning show from start to finish.

Consequently, what you pitch must be quick and to the point. Leave the investigative reporting to *Dateline* or *48 Hours* when viewers are prepared to sit through 30-minute segments. Also, if you think sitting there watching you be interviewed is going to enthrall viewers, think again. No one likes a talking head. If you're pitching something to a show, give the producer some additional material to work from. This could be video footage (B-roll), pictures, or whatever it is that can help add some flavor to your segment. While the average demographic will vary slightly from show to show, all of them are vying for the attention of women ages 18 to 49. If you can send them a bit that targets this specific market, you'll probably have a better chance of getting in the door.

Here's another key piece of advice: if your pitch doesn't fit on the back of a business card, you haven't refined it enough. Pitches that are lengthy won't get the attention of a producer. Confine your pitch to a quick, attention grabbing statement. Once you've piqued their interest, you can expand on your idea. Also, offer guests you know you can get in contact with and propose an entire segment rather than just a story idea. When you're set to pitch your story, be it to a small local station or a major national program, you'll need to remember to do one thing: Think like a producer. I do this whenever I'm pitching a client to a show. I start crafting my pitch by asking myself: "Why should they care?" What is it about your segment suggestion that could actually benefit the show? Forget for a moment that you'd like to get on national television and sell a million books. What is it about your topic that will interest their viewers? Ultimately, what's best for the show is all a good producer cares about. Finally, be excited about your topic. If the topic you're pitching doesn't register with you on some sort of emotional Richter scale, you can bet no one else will care about it either. Here are the shows and their guidelines:

The Today Show

Since *The Today Show* expanded their morning by one hour, they have opened the field considerably to additional topics. This includes authors and books. As the Literary Editor for The Today Show, Jackie Levin is responsible for booking interviews with authors. They don't always have to be well-known, but they do have to be able to speak well on television. Trusted topics include Parenting, Cooking, Self-Help, Personal Finance and Entertainment. If you can tie it into a hot news story, all the better. Send her a copy of the book and a letter with short bullet points, but don't send her a tape unless she asks.

When asked, send her a video of your author's previous appearances on TV, the book and a cover letter. Their lead-time is 6-8 months. She prefers nonfiction because they are news-driven. Once in a while they will promote a newcomer. Literary segments consist of author interviews and rarely, if ever, include reviews. Sports-related books are generally not featured unless they are newsworthy.

Jackie Levin, Producer
NBC News Today
30 Rockefeller Plaza, 3rd Floor
NYC, NY 10112
Phone: (212) 664-4371 or 1 (800) NBCNEWS, ext 4371.
Fax: (212) 664-7209
E-mail: Jaclyn.Levin@nbcuni.com

Media Tip!

If you're lucky enough to get on any morning show, don't try to sell your book on the air. Focus on giving a great interview, and who knows, you may get called back someday. Be generous with your information, be helpful, and offer solutions. Keep it professional.

Good Morning America

Patty Neger, Senior Segment Producer at GMA, says that she likes to see your packet first. Then, wait about three to four days before calling her back and never call her before 1:30 p.m. when the next day's show is in pre-production. The same holds true if you send a fax. Don't call the same day asking if she received it; give her a day or two to read it unless your topic ties into a hot story. In that case she'll want to hear from you right away. Patty also says she reads all of her e-mail and does, from time to time, consider pitches that are sent to her that way. One thing GMA will not consider featuring is fictional books.

Patty Neger, Book Editor and Senior Segment Producer
Good Morning America ABC-TV
147 Columbus Avenue, 6th Floor
New York, NY 10023
Phone: (212) 456-6157
Fax: (212) 456-7290
E-mail: patty.neger@abc.com

Pitching Tip!

When pitching your segment, you might try sending a packet to the show's topic-related expert. For example, John Nash is the aviation expert for *Good Morning America*. When you're pitching Patty Neger, you might want to send a copy of your book to John as well.

The Early Show

The Early Show's Kristin Matthews is always on the lookout for new authors and they do not discriminate against self-published authors. While the show does feature both novelists and nonfiction authors, their most popular topics are: personal finance, sports, living and health, general interest, and human interest.

Contact her initially by e-mail or U.S. mail. If you're going to call, do so after 11 a.m. and don't call on Friday afternoon. Keep in mind that authors are featured up to five times a week on this show, so this could be a great resource.

Kristin Matthews, Producer
CBS The Early Show
524 W. 57th Street
NYC, NY 10019
Phone: (212) 497-6022
Fax: (212) 975-2115
E-mail: krm@cbsnews.com or theearlyshow@cbsnews.com

Do's and Don'ts for Pitching the Morning Shows:

- Never, ever pitch the hosts

- Always, always double check your work for typos. Typographical errors are always a big turn off.

- If you can get guests to enhance your segment, mention that in your cover letter. But don't promise what you can't deliver.

- Unless noted otherwise, don't e-mail your pitch.

- Don't call on the biggest news day of the year unless your book is related to the breaking events.

Did you know?

Many media people have spam filters set up on their e-mail. To avoid getting your message sent straight to the trash bin, watch out for words that trigger spam filters on your recipient's e-mail. Words like "free" or "cash, cash, cash" or "make money fast!" will all trigger these filters and get your message deleted before it's even read. Also, DON'T USE CAPS UNLESS YOU'RE YELLING AT SOMEONE. Besides the fact that it's annoying, caps are also filter triggers.

Wall Street Journal - Weekender!

Have you read the Wall Street Journal over the weekend? Since Sept of 2005 they have been (very successfully) offering a weekend edition of their weekly newspaper. The Wall Street Journal "Weekend Journal" is great for soft news about culture, leisure, etc. Check out their Pursuits Section this Saturday and see where your story might fit!

GETTING ON OPRAH

Don't be afraid to go out on a limb. That's where the fruit is.
— H. Jackson Browne

So you think you're Oprah material, do you? Well, join the crowd. The mere mention of her name sends shivers down my spine. Since the demise of the original Oprah Book Club, the show needs to be your target for publicity. Her newest book club is tough to penetrate but there are myriad other ways to gain access to this show. Keep in mind that while many think Oprah is the brass ring, a visit to her show doesn't always ring the cash registers with book sales. In fact, I've seen some surprising numbers when it comes to sales, but remember, the cache of having been on her show can't be beat

Getting booked on *The Oprah Winfrey Show* has turned many unknown authors into tomorrow's superstars. It's the crown jewel, and it must be handled carefully.

Now, if you think that one book and one media kit's all it's going to take to get on her show, I've got news for you. It's been known to take as long as three years, or as short as a week. It all depends on you and what you're pitching and, it's important to know what has been chosen in the past. When pitching for the show, it's important to frequent the Web site (www2.oprah. com/index.jhtml), watch the show to see what's coming up, where their interests are and what producers might be looking for. There, you'll find listings of shows, past, present and future. There's even a call for guests that is updated frequently. Savvy self-promoters know to check this site often to see what guests the show might be looking for. We've known several people who have gotten on her show by being part of a show that was already in the works.

The books and topics chosen for the show are typically nonfiction in nature ranging in category from self-help, nutrition, family issues, relationships and everything in between.

But before you even think about approaching this show, get yourself some local media exposure first. Oprah will rarely feature someone who hasn't done media and there's a rigorous interview process to challenge all of your media skills. They want to be as certain as they can that they're not going to feature someone who will freeze on camera, or not have the kind of media presence the show needs.

One of the best ways to increase your chances of getting on the show is targeting the right people, it's been reported that this show gets upwards of 1,000 pitches a day, so the more focused you can make your pitch the better your chances of it getting noticed. Here is a very coveted list of the show's producers and their titles. Titles are very important and should be added to any correspondence with the show.

Send a copy of your book and media kit to each of them at the following address:

Harpo Productions
110 North Carpenter
Chicago, IL 60607
Phone: (312) 633-0808

Executive Producer:
Ellen Rakieten
Senior Supervising Producers:
Katy Murphy Davis
Dana Newton-Utigard

Senior Producer:
Lisa Morin

Producers:
Laura Grant Sillars
Jill Barancik
John Bukalow
Jennifer Kinnear Stamper
Jill Von Lokeren-Kuenstler
Amy Coleman
Lisa Erspamer
Jack Mori
Susan Russo
April Terrien
Caroline Ziv

Senior associate producers:
Jill Adams
Dana Brooks
Candi Carter
Terry Goulder
James Kelley
Jenna Kostelnik
Lesia Minor
Tara Montgomery

Other associate producers:
Teresa Aquilera
Heather Aldridge
Ray Dotch
Leslie Grisanti
Suzanne Hayward
Becky Liscum
Gregg Sherkin
Stacy Strazi
Andrea Wishom

Know that if you send something directly to Oprah, she probably won't peruse it herself unless it has made it past her front-line of producers. She has an army of producers and assistants that weed through the huge amounts of mail and books they receive. Two producers who should be at the top of your list are Katy Murphy Davis and Ellen Rakieten.

So what *is* the real secret for getting on the show? Well, that might be a better kept secret than the Colonel's herbs and spices. There is, however, one common thread you should consider. First, never assume that your book is show-worthy and don't mark your package that way. Just put together a professional media kit, include a copy of your book and send it off. I will reiterate: don't mark the outside with *"The Oprah Show,"* that's the quickest way for your book to land up in never-never land. In the end, perhaps the biggest secret to getting on her show is no secret at all: Oprah must love your book and topic. That's it, bottom line. Despite what her producers might encourage her to do, if Oprah doesn't love it, you won't see it on her show.

Can't get on Oprah? Why not start your own TV show? Just about every city in the U.S. has something called a "community access" channel. Call you local cable provider and get the number, tell them of your expertise or the idea for your show. They will usually have you go through a programming class or two, and then, you're off and running! Watch out, Oprah!

Every e-mail you send could be ruining your marketing campaign.

The most crucial bit of pitching information you could get might be about your e-mail. Why? Because long, lengthy e-mails won't get read and certainly won't get noticed, and many times, they might get you a one-way ticket into an e-mail trash bin. Remember the "above the fold" rule, which is an old newspaper term. Everything of importance is always "above the fold" of the paper, and your e-mails should be the same. Keep your pitch to the top half of an e-mail; don't make a reporter or producer scroll through your message to find the hook. Keep your message short and to the point and remember, never ever sell your book – always sell what the book can do for the reader, listener, and viewer.

CONTACTING THE ASSOCIATED PRESS

Journalism is merely history's first draft.
— Geoffrey C. Ward

Stories written by the *Associated Press* (the world's largest media organization) reach over 1,500 daily and weekly newspapers and countless TV and radio stations around the globe. Known for its breaking news coverage, this news service has over 235 bureaus worldwide. You can pitch them like you would any other media contact. The caveat here is that your story MUST have a strong national or international appeal. You can of course pitch your state bureau with state-specific news and they will consider that as well. The best way to pitch your AP office is via fax. Most offices house only a few employees, making phone pitches too time consuming. The list below is a smattering of the bureaus around the country. If you don't see one listed for your town, call one of the other offices to see if they can refer you. Or check your local listings. Bureau Chiefs are listed by each as your primary contact. If no Bureau Chief is listed, call them for the name of their News Editor. Here are the offices around the country:

Austin Bureau
1005 Congress Avenue, Suite 995
Austin, TX 78701-2469
Phone: (512) 472-4004
Fax: (512) 469-0800
Correspondent: Kelley Shannon

Chicago Bureau
10 S. Wacker Drive, Ste 2500
Chicago, IL 60606-7491
Phone: (312) 781-0500
Fax: (312) 781-1989
Bureau Chief: Bill Handy

Dallas Bureau
4851 Lyndon B. Johnson Freeway, Suite 300
Dallas, TX 75244-6047 6002
Phone: (972) 991-2100
Fax: (972) 991-7207
Bureau Chief: Dale Leach

Denver Bureau
1444 Wazee Street, Suite 130
Denver, CO 80202-1395
Phone: (303) 825-0123
Fax: (303) 892-5927
Bureau Chief: George Garties

Houston Bureau
16945 Northchase Drive, Suite 2110
Houston, TX 77060-2151

Phone: (281) 872-8900
Fax: (281) 872-9988
Bureau Chief: Wendy Benjaminson

Las Vegas Bureau
300 S. 4th St., Ste
Las Vegas, NV 89101
Phone: (702) 382-7440
Fax: (702) 382-0790
News Editor: Tom Tait (Their bureau chief is in LA)

Los Angeles Bureau
221 S. Figueroa Street, Suite 300
Los Angeles, CA 90012-2553
Phone: (213) 626-1200
Fax: (213) 346-0200
Bureau Chief/Editor: Justin Pritchard

New York Bureau
450 West 33rd Street
New York, NY 10020-1605 --10001
Phone: (212) 621-1500 – (212) 621-1670
Fax: (212) 621-7520
Bureau Chief: Howard Goldberg

Philadelphia Bureau
1835 Market Street, Ste 1700
Philadelphia, PA 19103-2945
Phone: (215) 561-1133
Fax: (215) 561-3544
Bureau Chief: Sally Carpenter Hale

Phoenix Bureau
1850 N. Central Ave., Ste 640
Phoenix, AZ 85004
Phone: (602) 258-8934
Fax: (602) 254-9573
Bureau Chief: Linda Wienandt

Portland Bureau
121 SW Salmon Street, Suite 1450
Portland, OR 97204-2924
Phone: (503) 228-2169
Fax: (503) 228-5514
Bureau Chief: Bryan Brumley

San Diego Bureau
350 Camino De La Reina
San Diego, CA 92108-2098
Phone: (619) 231-3587
Fax: (619) 291-2098
Correspondent: Michelle Morgante

San Francisco Bureau
303 Second Street, Ste 680 N
San Francisco, CA 94107
Phone: (415) 495-1708
Fax: (415) 495-4967 – (415) 495-5062
Bureau Chief: John Raess

Seattle Bureau
3131 Elliott Ave, Ste 750
Seattle, WA   98121-1095

Phone: (206) 682-1812
Fax: (206) 621-1948
Bureau Chief: Nancy Trott

Washington D.C. Bureau
2021 K Street NW, Ste 600
Washington, DC 20006-1003 –
Phone: (202) 776-9400
Fax: (202) 776-9570
Bureau Chief: Sandy Johnson

Marketing Tip

USA Today is publishing a new e-mail newsletter about books. A weekly gossip column by USA Today's Bob Minzesheimer is called "Hot Type." Send him your info via e-mail to bminzesheimer@usatoday.com

SYNDICATE YOURSELF

Writing is an occupation in which you have to keep
proving your talent to those who have none.
—Jules Renard

Over the years I've spoken to a number of authors who say they aspire to write a syndicated column. Getting syndicated is a great idea, albeit a challenging one. If you've thought of this no doubt most (if not all) of your competition has too. But don't let this discourage you; while syndication may take a while, it's still worth pursuing.

There are a number of tried and true ways you can enter this market; there are also a few "back door" methods that might work equally as well. The first thing you'll need to do, however, is get to know your competition. For this I recommend that you get a copy of The Editor & Publisher "Annual Directory of Syndication." Sometimes you can get this in bookstores but I'd recommend just ordering it online at www.editorandpublisher. com. Explore this book carefully and you'll find that syndicated columns are listed by both the syndication service that offers them as well as their topic. This will give you a good starting point in your research and since most newspapers now have on-line archives, you'll be able to explore past articles and see how these topics differ from your own.

Once you've explored this, define for yourself how your topic/angle is different from the ones you found during your research. Then once you've defined this, you can start targeting papers or syndication services with your query letter and sample articles. This is the traditional way of entering this market. For most it can be long and tedious and you might find that without prior "clippings" to offer, the process takes even longer. In that vein, I'd recommend that you try offering your column locally first or to one paper at a time not in a "syndication deal" but as a filler; newspapers will be a lot quicker to take filler items than to explore syndication options with you. By offering them consistent filler content (and saving those valuable clippings) you'll start to grow your level of experience, you'll build a reputation with the editor or editorial staff and you'll begin to get a sense of what does and doesn't work with printed media. An associate of mine did this, not with a local paper but with a paper she'd been offering her articles to; after about two years of consistent submissions she may be in line to fill the shoes of their in-house syndicated columnist who is retiring.

Once you have built some exposure for yourself and gathered clippings of your work, then it's time to start pitching your topic to syndicated services (some of them are listed below) or regional newspapers. For this you'll need a great query letter that establishes your credentials and explains why your idea is different from the others they might be considering. You'll need some sample articles (other than your clippings) and perhaps some letters of reference from some papers you've worked for. Submit this packet to newspapers or syndicated services that might be appropriate for your topic and then keep good records; do your follow-up just like you would if you were pitching the media on anything else. The same rules apply really: pitch and follow-up and stay on their radar screen.

So, at the end of the day when you find yourself successfully syndicated will you get paid for all your hard work? Absolutely! What you'll get paid varies depending on how many papers feature you and whether you are working through a syndication service. Syndication services are great but they will typically take 40 to 50 percent of your sales. If you self-syndicate you get all the proceeds. While it's great to self-syndicate, keep in mind that you'll need to have good tracking systems in place once your column takes off.

As a published author, syndication can be another great way to promote you and your book. Your book will lend you the credibility you need to get that column and from this ongoing printed exposure some lucrative publishing deals could follow suit. Syndication may not be an easy road but if tackled correctly, it can be a great way to boost your promotion, expand your platform and get the kind of exposure you only dreamed of!

Major syndicates - check online for their submission guidelines

Copley News Service
http://www.copleynews.com

King Features
http://www.kingfeatures.com

Universal Press Syndicate
http://www.amuniversal.com/ups/index.htm

Bonus Tip: If you're trying to follow the comings and goings of syndicated writers, Editor and Publisher (www. editorandpublisher) is a great resource for that. Check out the "Departments" tab on their Web site for the latest news on columns that might be coming available!

An Audience of Seventy-Five Million

Want to reach 75 million people in one shot? How about pitching Parade Magazine? You know the one you get with your Sunday paper? They accept pitches and freelance work. Here's how to get your stuff in front of them.

Parade magazine relishes the unusual. In fact, they've done stories on an elephant sanctuary and people who dance with their dogs. The bottom line is if your story doesn't make you happy or sad, angry, or elated, chances are Parade readers won't care and neither will their Editorial staff.

Parade is also looking for news, but this term is used very loosely by them because of their four week lead time on stories. Don't bother pitching poetry, fiction, travel stories, or quizzes. The best way to sell yourself to Parade is to establish a niche and be specific about your area of expertise.

Contact their offices to get the name of the person you should be pitching to and make sure to check out their Web site!

Parade

711 3rd Avenue

New York, NY 10017-4038

Phone: (212) 450-7000

Web site: www.parade.com

RADIO, REACHING FOR THE MASSES

Writing is like prostitution. First you do it for love,
then for a few close friends, and finally for money.
— Unknown

How can you reach millions of people without ever leaving your home? Why, radio, of course. As our commutes grow longer, we spend more time in our cars than ever before. We live in a very virtual society. We often don't know our neighbor but yet we still need to feel connected somehow. That's where radio comes in.

There are two types of radio interviews. The first is in-studio, which means exactly that. You go into the studio and get to meet with the host directly. The second is called phone-in or "phoners." This means that you can take the call in your robe and slippers if you want to, and no one will be the wiser. My recommendation is to be comfortable, but be prepared. Sometimes making the call from your home can seem like you're just talking on the phone to a friend. Keep in mind that you are still speaking to the masses, even if you are wearing bunny slippers. I was telling a friend of mine the other day that I was interviewed on a radio station in Hawaii. "Wow," she said, "you got to go to Hawaii. How exciting!" Well exciting yes, but to tell the truth I never set foot in Hawaii to do this interview. I sat here in my office, my feet propped up on the desk talking with a DJ who had graciously agreed to interview me.

Most radio stations use "phoners" and most guests love appearing on radio this way. Did you know that there are more than 1,400 radio talk shows that need guests on a constant basis? If you're willing to do your research, I guarantee there's a radio show (or shows) perfect for your topic.

There are a lot of pros and cons about radio interviews. First of all, you're probably going to get more time on radio than you would on television. And, while television is visual, when you're on radio you'll get a better chance to expand on your subject matter and get across exactly what you want to say. If you live in the city where the interview takes place, then I recommend that you go to the studio if at all possible.

Did you know? On an average day U.S. radio stations book more than 10,000 guests.

When you position yourself for radio, don't discriminate against some of the smaller cities. Many people will just want to pitch the bigger markets and largest shows and while this is certainly admirable, you'll end up overlooking a great deal of quality programming. As a matter of fact, unless you feel the program or radio demographic is not in your best interest, I wouldn't turn down any offer to speak on radio. Every time you get to do a program, you are honing your skills. You get better every time, and with luck, by the time you hit a huge demographic – you'll be an absolute pro.

Now, when pitching yourself for radio, keep one thing in mind. You're the expert and you're providing a solution. If you can solve people's problems, they will love you. If your book provides a solution, great! If it doesn't, then find the story or the controversy behind the book, or promote the story behind the author. The book, at this point, might even become secondary. Keep that in mind when you're pitching the stations. While your book might not be of particular interest to the show's producer, how you sell it must be.

When I was trying to garner media attention for *The Cliffhanger*, I realized that romantic fiction might not get me on the airwaves, but the publishing story behind it could. So I began to develop a plan, a well-thought-out promotional campaign based on the method of publishing (the new print-on-demand publishing revolution) as opposed to the book itself. The book at that point became less of a statement and more of an example of what discouraged authors can do to promote themselves. It worked! There was a huge amount of interest in this particular subject, and while I still sold my books, it was more out of curiosity for the product rather than its content.

When you are speaking on the air, don't sound too canned. And don't sound like a politician. Rehearsed speeches will come over just that way. And most of us don't have the proper training to take a rehearsed speech and make it sound natural. Know your stuff and speak like the authority you are. Always remember: you're there to share your message, offer a solution and sell your book.

One of the best pieces of advice someone ever gave me was "Be enthusiastic!" If you're not excited about your product or your message, how can you expect your listener to be? Also, make a list of a few points you want to make and keep making them through your talk. Keep in mind that if you're recording this in advance, some of what you say will get edited out so you want to make your most vital statements enough so that they have a chance to be heard. It might not even be a bad idea to have a mission statement or index cards with your points listed on them so you can keep referring back to them throughout your interview.

Now, of course, even though your book might be secondary as we discussed above, you still want to get people interested in it. How about creating a highlight sheet or tip sheet from your talk and faxing it to anyone who calls in to request it? That way you can include your book's information on the sheet as well. If they like your tip sheet, they'll most likely order the book.

So, now that you're ready for radio... how to get on the air? Well, a good place to start is Radiospace.com. This site will link you to radio shows and stations across the country. It's a great resource if you're pitching an idea and can't figure out where to go. Click on Programming Resources, this will take you directly to their list of stations and syndicated programs.

Tips for a Successful Radio Interview

• Assume that you're on the air as soon as you pick up the phone. Often the host or producer will call you and you'll instantly be "live," so be prepared!

- Don't assume the host will read your book; they rarely do this! Make sure to send a one-page synopsis with your book and press kit.

- Even though you've included some great questions with your press kit, don't assume they will use them – be prepared for whatever they might ask you!

- Don't be long-winded. Rehearse your questions beforehand; keep your answers concise and don't venture off into tangents that will distract the audience and lose valuable momentum.

- Try to listen to the station and the show you're going to be on ahead of time. You can often do this from their Web site but if nothing else, you can always call the station during the program and ask to be put on hold.

- Sit up straight or stand up when you speak. Slouching will cause you to sound less dynamic.

- Keep an eye on the clock. If your interview is 15 minutes, know that you will need to start the wrap-up and perhaps a brief three-point recap of your talk two minutes prior to ending the call.

How to be a Fantastic Radio Guest!

1) If you're doing an interview in a city that's not your own try familiarizing yourself with their news climate. Try to tie your story or interview into something that's got a local angle

2)   Don't push your political views on the show unless
      appropriate, especially if you're unfamiliar with the
      city's political climate

3)   Never, ever use a cell phone to do an interview

4)   Be yourself! Don't try and manufacture a persona,
      listeners will see right through that.

Make Every Interview Count

If you're able to get the radio or television interview,
make sure to tape it or get a copy. Armed with that, you can
now get the interview digitized (transferred to CD). Once it's
transferred, it's a lot easier to include a CD in your press kit
than a bulky tape. If you have a computer with a CD burner
all the better. You can burn your own CD's, make labels for
them and you've got another great looking piece of marketing
material to include with your media kits. Not only that, but
you can also attach a digitized copy of your interview to the
pressroom on your Web site. That way people can go online
and hear your interview as well.

Radio Tip

Don't forget! Bring a cassette tape to the studio or send one
in advance if you're going to be a "phoner." This really came
in handy for me when I was doing an in-studio spot during a
book tour in Oregon. It was a small station and they did not

record any of their programming. Thankfully, I was able to whip out my tape recorder and I had a copy of the show. Good thing because it turned out to be a great program.

How to get on radio...tomorrow

Pitch a Holiday:

I can't tell you how many interviews my company books when we have a holiday hook. Dozens and dozens of requests pour into our office for bookings before, during and the week after the holiday. When you're pitching a holiday, your initial thought might be to pitch the obvious topics. But if you can put a non-traditional twist on a traditional idea, you've probably just guaranteed yourself a radio interview. For example, during Valentine's Day everyone wants to talk about dating, keeping love alive and meeting Mr. Right. But what can you offer that would be different? Here are some recent topics we've offered to shows. See if any of them spark your interest, or perhaps help you ignite an idea of your own:

- The Top Three Things People DON'T do that Screws up Their Marriages

- What's the Hottest New Place to Find Love this Valentine's Day? How about a soup kitchen!

- Sweetheart Secrets to Make Your Valentine's Day Sizzle; Simple steps to rekindle the romance!

Pitching a News Topic

If you can tie your topic into something going on in the news, you can nearly double your chances of getting on radio. Watch your local news or morning shows, read the paper from cover to cover and see what you can comment on. Or, maybe it's a different spin on an existing issue. Reality TV is a biggie these days, can you speak to that? If your book is all about relationships, this might be a perfect opportunity for you to get on radio.

Pitching with Pizzazz

When pitching radio, I put together what I call my guest "one sheets." These one sheets are simple one page releases with a catchy headline, a snappy intro, and a bullet point list of "talking points" my guest can speak to (don't forget the contact information). When you're pitching radio, especially morning shows, make this one sheet fun! Don't hesitate to get creative with it as long as it fits in with your topic. The more creative and eye-catching you get, the better your chances of getting called back.

Follow Up

If you're submitting your one sheet to many shows at the same time, it's often not necessary to follow up. Our team will usually just send a fax over and let the station contact us if they're interested.

A Match Made in Media Heaven

Because I've been able to clearly define an audience for any particular guest I offer, the ratio of bookings is very high. If you've been sending out pitches with little response, consider reevaluating who your audience really is. If your topic isn't morning drive time material, send it to an afternoon or evening show. Know the limitations of what you're promoting and decide where it fits in. Knowing this will double your chances of getting scheduled on a program. If you can, listen to the show you're pitching. If the station is in another state, log onto their Web site to see if you can hear what the program sounds like. If they don't offer audio streaming, remember that you can always call the station and ask to be put on hold! Five to 10 minutes of listening to their show will give you a good idea of their format.

Be Helpful

It's important to know that while you're promoting your topic, the first order of business is to offer assistance and helpful advice to their listeners. Be very, very generous with your tips, ideas, and suggestions.

Go For the Syndicates

If you want to get on several stations at once, pitch a syndicated show. There are hundreds of them to choose from all around the country. You might even consider pitching radio news broadcasters. If you get an item picked up for news inserts it will get repeated several times throughout the day!

Timing

When you pitch is often crucial to getting picked up. Depending on the show and the size of the station, you could get a same day interview or be scheduled weeks out. Usually, the larger the show the longer the lead-time. If you're planning on targeting a holiday, start with a first round of faxes a month out. As you get within the two-week range, send them again.

One, Two, Three, Pitch

Unlike many televisions programs and news shows that won't feature their competitor's information, radio stations usually don't have this policy. Unless you're targeting a station like NPR (with competitive programming), you won't run the risk of getting overlooked just because you've been on a different station.

A Few Pitch Potentials

There are a number of things that you might be able to pitch to. Consider Easter, Memorial Day, Mother's Day and Father's Day, Independence Day, the summer vacation season, back to school, Thanksgiving, Christmas, and military holidays. All of these offer a myriad of great angles for pitch potential. For example, while the summer vacation season might seem like a travel heavy topic, why not pitch something a bit different. Did you know that the amount of people who get lost in the wilderness doubles during the month of July? If you have a book on survival in the wilderness, this might be a perfect time for you pitch yourself to radio.

Best Times to Pitch

There are certain times of the year that are better than others for pitching radio. Whenever possible, I always try to 'feed' the media during times when I know they'll be hungry for news and guests. Some of the best times I've found for pitching are during holidays and vacations. The week between Christmas and New Year's for example, is excellent, as are the summer months. Another great time? Federal holidays when news is almost guaranteed to slow down.

And finally, consider doing an author tour without ever leaving your office! How? Well, radio of course! Ninety-five percent of the people I book on radio do interviews from the comfort of their own home.

"See" you on the airwaves!

Searching for stations in your area? Then head on over to the following links.

For a listing of AM stations: www.fcc.gov/mb/audio/amq. html

For a listing of FM stations: www.fcc.gov/mb/audio/fmq. html

Another great radio locater is www.radio-locator.com

NATIONAL PUBLIC RADIO

Outside of a dog, a book is a man's best friend.
Inside of a dog, it's too dark to read.
— Groucho Marx

From my perspective, National Public Radio (NPR) is a gold mine. If you've spent any time listening to their broadcasts (and I highly encourage you to do this), you'll note that they not only offer very thorough reporting, but also give their audience a very wide variety of programs from which to choose. From *Car Talk* to *Talk of the Nation*, the possibilities are endless. At last report, they had a listener base of 19.3 million with 600 affiliate stations nationwide. Before you pitch anyone on the list below, listen to their program. As with anything, you'll want to cater your pitch. Once you've determined who you want to contact, send them a copy of your book with a pitch letter detailing why this book would be perfect featured on their show. If you're pitching an issue, it's always an added bonus if you can pitch something that was featured on their program (as a follow-up topic) or something that might be a current news story. As with any medium, their shows need lead-time so send them an advance copy whenever possible. And keep in mind that some of the NPR folks will not feature someone who has already been interviewed on another show. When you're pitching, send your media kit to as many as you

feel are appropriate to your topic but know that once it's been
featured, that's probably it for a while. Once, however, may be
all you need.

Morning Edition
Ellen McDonnell, Executive Producer
Jim Wallace, Book Review Producer
635 Massachusetts Avenue, NW
Washington, DC 20001
Phone: (202) 513-2150
Fax: (202) 513-3040
E-mail: Emcdonnell@npr.org
E-mail: Jwallace@npr.org

Show format: One of the premier programs on American
radio today celebrating its 20th anniversary as NPR's flagship
morning news program. They feature: current events, business,
sports, and history. Four 10 minute segments each day. Pitching
advice: One sure-fire way to get blacklisted is to leave Jim a
voicemail message. You can e-mail him your pitch initially,
then follow up to see if there's an interest. You might go ahead
and tell him in your e-mail that you're going to send him a
book and media kit. It's rare that Jim will feature a book on his
show. More often than not, their guests are issue related.

All Things Considered
Carol Klinger, Booker
635 Massachusetts Avenue, NW
Washington, DC 20001
Phone: (202) 513-2107
Fax: (202) 424-3329
E-mail: atc@npr.org

Show format: One of the oldest and most listened to programs, *All Things Considered* runs on approximately 570 stations nationwide Monday through Friday. This two-hour program has a weekly audience of 11 million. All Things Considered offers listeners a timely, intelligent look at the day's news as well as newsmaker interviews, arts, books, film, theatre and everything in-between. Pitching advice: Try not to pitch by phone. If you must call, do so before 10 a.m. or after 4 p.m. Pitch by mail initially, then call to follow-up. She also loves to hear about emerging authors, so get your story to her.

Weekend, All Things Considered
Davar Ardalan, Producer
635 Massachusetts Avenue, NW
Washington, DC 20001
Phone: (202) 513-2140
Fax: (202) 513-3029
E-mail: dardalan@npr.org

Show format: This show will feature one or two authors and airs Saturday and Sunday. Much like *All Things Considered*, they offer listeners a timely look at current events. Pitching advice: Davar must see your book so don't send your media kit without it. Give her a chance to peruse it, then call to check and see if she's received it. Or, you can e-mail her initially; follow up with your press kit and then call.

Talk of the Nation
Ellen Silva, Producer
Susan Lund, Booker
635 Massachusetts Avenue, NW

Washington, DC 20001
Phone: (202) 513-2340
Fax: (202) 513-3031
E-mail: esilva@npr.org
E-mail: slund@npr.org

Show format: This news-driven talk show provides in-depth, intelligent and thought-provoking discussion on the day's hot topics. This show is syndicated in Europe and runs eight times per week. They do feature authors, sometimes one every day. They run The Book Club the second to last Thursday of every month. They like diversity in their authors and will sometimes announce their authors weeks in advance. See what I mean about advance copies? Pitching advice: Even though I stress advance copies, try not to send your media kit naked. She usually won't consider something that is fresh off the press unless it's already garnered a heap of buzz. Include some reviews and press clippings with your packet. Also, given the show, make sure your pitch is topical and newsworthy!

News & Notes with Ed Gordon
Nicole Childers, Producer Phone: (310) 815-4378,
nchilders@npr.org
801 2nd Ave Rm 701
New York, NY   10017-8642
Phone: (212) 878-1430
Fax: (212) 878-1429

Show Format: A daily national news talk program exploring headlines, issues, trends and newsmakers from an African-American perspective. Ed Gordon takes the mainstream story and gives it context in this new program distributed to NPR affiliates nationwide.

Fresh Air with Terry Gross
Amy Salit, Producer
150 N. Sixth Street
Philadelphia, PA 19106
Phone: (215) 351-9200
Fax: (215) 574-1477
E-mail: asalit@whyy.org

Show format: The show offers a mixed bag of information with an open ended format. This allows for a broad swath of topics from arts and entertainment to news-driven topics of the day. *Fresh Air* is best known for its captivating interviews with guests from the world of literature, science, music, film, and more. *Fresh Air* is broadcast nationally over 294 stations and abroad via World Radio Network. The show reaches over 2 million listeners a week. Typically, Amy is open to any topic and won't rule out anything initially. Interviews on this show can run as long as an hour. Pitch yourself, not the book. Pitching advice: Amy likes a lot of information. Don't forget to include your resume, any news clippings and previous interviews if you have them digitized.

Weekend Edition Saturday
Sarah Beyer-Kelly, Producer
Peter Breslow, Senior Producer
635 Massachusetts Avenue, NW
Washington, DC 20001
Phone: (202) 513-2270

Fax: (202) 513-3029
E-mail: wesat@npr.org
E-mail: pbreslow@npr.org

Show format: News, interviews, and feature stories are
the flavor of the day for *Weekend Edition Saturday*. The
show's host, Scott Simon, likes pop-culture and enlightening
nonfiction. He's also interested in anything on Chicago,
Quakerism, baseball and spirituality. Anything that is unusual
will pique his curiosity as well. A portion of the show is news
related but they also cover some very bizarre issues as well.
Pitching advice: All staff members are accessible and will
consider pitches sent via e-mail.

Weekend Edition Sunday
Neil Carruth, Story Assistant Editor
635 Massachusetts Avenue, NW
Washington, DC 20001
Phone: (202) 513-2880
Fax: (202) 513-3060
E-mail: ncarruth@npr.org

Show format: With news, interviews, and feature stories,
Weekend Edition Sunday covers the gamut. They include
popular culture, Internet commentators, and special segments
and they welcome authors of all kinds as long as their topic
is show-appropriate. *Weekend Edition Sunday* is known for
their relaxed, listener-friendly show format and they always
welcome the opportunity to go after the unusual. While most of
their topics are serious they will occasionally go after a funny
segment.

Pitching advice: Send Neil an e-mail pitch first, then follow up to see if there's an interest before you send him more material. Depending on the subject matter and segment, he might have specific items he will need to see before making his decision.

The Diane Rehm Show
Elizabeth Terry, Producer
WAMU-FM
4000 Brandywine Street, NW
Washington, DC 20016
Phone: (202) 885-1231
E-mail: eterry@wamu.org

Show format: A public affairs and call-in program which analyzes the news and examines issues that affect our daily lives. Produced by WAMU in Washington, DC, guests range from Archbishop Desmond Tutu and Gloria Steinem, to John Updike and Maya Angelou. Pitching advice: They like to interview authors right when their book comes out but don't want to be pitched on author-related topics by phone. Instead pitch producer Elizabeth Terry by e-mail or send her a copy of your book when it's released. Diane Rehm likes to do the first interview and won't follow *Talk of the Nation* or *Public Interest*. They will, however, consider an author who's been on Fresh Air.

Living on Earth
Eileen Bolinsky, Executive Producer
20 Holland Street, Ste 408
Somerville, MA 02144-2749

Phone: (617) 629-3626
Fax: (617) 629-2625
E-mail: bolinsky@loe.org

Show format: If you have an environment-related issue this show is for you. The multi-award winning program with host Steve Curwood, explores our environment, what we're doing to it, and what it's doing to us. In-depth coverage, features, interviews, and commentary examine how the environment affects medicine, politics, technology, economics, transportation, agriculture, and more.

Bookworm KCRW-FM
Melinda Seigel, Producer
1900 Pico Blvd.
Santa Monica, CA, 90405
Phone: (310) 450-5183
Fax: (310) 450-7172
E-mail: Seagull35@aol.com

Show Format: Weekly interview program featuring books and authors in genres of literary fiction and poetry. They are interested in emerging authors as well as established names. The station is based in Santa Monica and welcomes in-studio guests as well as phoners. You'll want to first check out their Web site at www.kcrw.org to make sure your book is a match for their programming. Pitching advice: To submit books for consideration, send a copy of the book along with your press kit. Do not follow-up on your submission. If the host, Michael Silverblatt, is interested, he will get back to you. If he likes something, he gets right on it.

Latino USA
Alex Avila, Senior Producer
Communications Bldg B UT-Austin
Austin, TX 78712
Phone: (512) 471-6178
Fax: (512) 475-6873
E-mail: avila@mail.utexas.edu

Show format: *Latino USA* is a weekly show that provides public radio audiences with information about the issues and events that affect the lives of one of the nation's largest growing demographics. *Latino USA* consists of weekly news roundups, public affairs and cultural segments to promote a cross-cultural understanding. Pitching advice: Pitch via e-mail only and allow a 10-day lead-time for someone to get back with you.

On the Media
WNYC Radio
One Centre St.
24th Floor
New York, NY 10007
onthemedia@wnyc.org – use this for pitches, do not contact a producer directly

Show format: Weekly magazine program which examines the interplay between media and American society. The host leads provocative conversations with some of the biggest personalities in the field on a variety of topics ranging from journalistic accuracy to the effects of prime time TV on our culture to the power of the Internet.

Verify Everything!

The quickest way to have your press release or media kit hit the circular file is to have it addressed to someone who left to go to the competitor. I've noticed that often names I had for media contacts as little as two months ago might no longer be good, so double check everything. It only takes a quick phone call and you can rest assured that your packet or press release will end up in the right hands, instead of someone's trash can.

Seconds Matter (when pitching the media)

Did you know that studies have shown that newsroom reporters spend an average of five seconds reading your pitch before deciding to follow-up or skipping to the next pitch? Seconds matter when pitching the media, so what will you do with your five seconds? Send them a strong pitch and great angle that pulls them in from the start and keeps you from getting round-filed when your five seconds are up.

The Best Day to Pitch

Ok, so we've all heard that the worst day in the world to make pitching or sales calls is Monday, right? Wrong. Turns out you'll find more people in the office on a Monday than on any other day of the week. If you're broadcasting a news release Tuesday, Wednesday and Thursday are the best days to do this. Avoid Fridays as many clipping services don't pick up Friday releases or don't pick them up until Saturday; some news sources use these to review information for potential stories

SERIOUS SATELLITE RADIO

On CBS Radio the news of Ed Murrow's death, reportedly
from lung cancer, was followed by a cigarette commercial.
— Alexander Kendrick

The dynamics of media are changing drastically. TiVo has
changed the way we watch TV and satellite radio has changed
the dial on AM/FM, maybe for good. Regardless of what you
believe or don't believe relative to the staying power of satellite
radio, one thing is for sure. The power the consumer now has to
tune out commercials and have access to hundreds of stations
cannot be understated and will likely change radio forever.

There are two giants in the satellite industry. XM Radio and
Sirius Satellite radio currently dominate the scene. Each boasts
a steady stream of music and talk, but XM it would seem, tops
out at having the most stations (including talk). Sirius has 125
while XM has 160 to their credit. Sirius is probably best known
for their coup of luring Howard Stern away from traditional
radio to the satellite world, but they also have Martha Stewart
and several other talk programs. To compete, XM announced
in 2005 that it had closed a $55 million deal to get Oprah on
its nationwide airwaves. "Oprah and Friends" is set to debut in
September of 2006, and Good Morning America just launched

the radio version of its morning show too, giving XM quite a bit of buzz. When satellite radio first came on the scene it seemed like a novelty, something that would fade in time. But now, some three years into the satellite craze, the listener base seems to be widening and with more and more new cars being sold with satellite radio already built in, the choice for many is clear. Most consumers will listen to a mix of traditional and satellite radio so pitching both makes sense. How do you pitch this type of radio? The same way you'd pitch traditional radio. Listen to their show, get a sense of their format and then contact the producer or host (depending on who takes pitches). If you're not a subscriber to satellite radio and wonder how you can listen to a show you might want to check their individual Web sites. Often you can subscribe to their webcasting that will allow you to listen to programming via the Internet; this way you can listen to the shows a few times without incurring the cost of the sign-up and equipment. You can visit their respective Web sites at: www.xmradio.com and www.sirius. com. Here is a sampling of the shows on both stations that welcome pitches from authors.

The XM Radio Lineup
The XM address:
1500 Eckington Place, NE
Washington DC 20007

Pitching tip: When mailing to XM, please put the producer's name, name of the show, and then the address.

The Opie and Anthony Show
1500 Eckington Pl NE, Ste 2

Washington, DC 20002-2164
Phone: (202) 380-4000
Fax: (202) 380-4500
E-mail: feedback@opieandanthony.com
Homepage: www.opieandanthony.com

XM's answer to Howard Stern might be The Opie and
Anthony Show. Pegged as an entertainment show, the hosts are
known for their cutting-edge and outrageous style. Their target
audience is listeners 18 thru 34 and they prefer live interviews.
Send your press releases, books or products to the following
people:

Mr. Anthony Cumia, Producer
Phone: (212) 830-3717
Fax: (202) 380-4500
anthony@opieandanthony.com (p)

Mr. Rick Delgado, Producer
Phone: (212) 830-3714
Fax: (202) 380-4500
E-mail: rick@wnew.com

Mr. Gregg Hughes, Producer
Phone: (212) 830-3714
Fax: (202) 380-4500
E-mail: opie@opieandanthony.com (p)

The Bob Edwards Show
1500 Eckington Pl NE, Ste 2
Washington, DC 20002-2164
Phone: (202) 380-4800
Fax: (202) 380-4801

Bob Edwards provides listeners with insightful, entertaining and provocative programming produced by some of the most respected names in public broadcasting. Partners include Public Radio International (PRI) and its station partners Chicago Public Radio and WGBH Boston; American Public Media (the production and distribution arm of Minnesota Public Radio); and Boston public radio station WBUR. This show airs daily at 8 a.m. EST and then rebroadcasts at 9 a.m. EST, 10 a.m. EST and 8 p.m. EST. Their target audience is listeners ages 18 through 34. Send your press releases, books or products to the following individual:

Ms. Andy Danyo, Producer
Phone: (202) 380-4822
Fax: (202) 380-4801
E-mail: andy.danyo@xmradio.com

Pitching tips: Danyo is responsible for booking guests, conducting preliminary interviews, screening listener calls, researching show topics and reviewing all press submissions as Producer.

Life Love & Health
741 Tehama St
San Francisco, CA 94103-3822
Phone: (415) 663-8428
E-mail: info@lifeloveandhealth.com
Homepage: www.lifeloveandhealth.com

Life Love & Health provides health and wellness information with celebrity stories and human drama. Life Love & Health requests that those interested in the program first listen to samples at the Web site before submitting pitches.

Their segments run 90 seconds on various channels at various times throughout the day. They do not like phone calls and strongly encourage authors to listen to the show first before pitching. Send your press releases, books or products to the following individual:

> Mr. Christopher Springmann, Host/Producer
> Phone: (415) 663-8428
> Fax: (202) 380-4500
> E-mail: info@lifeloveandhealth.com

Mimi Geerges Show
PO Box 267
Oakton, VA 22124-0267
Phone: (703) 251-3002
E-mail: info@mgshow.org
Homepage: www.mgshow.org

An independently produced talk radio program that features interviews with the country's leading experts, authors, scientists and entertainers. The program presents a diversity of views on a wide array of topics. It strives to provide listeners with the information and insight to form their own views and opinions. Note that their lead times for news items are often 30 days prior to the air date. The show airs on Sunday from 9 to 10 p.m. Send your press releases, books or products to the following people:

> Ms. Mimi Geerges, Host/Executive Producer
> Phone: (703) 251-3002
> Fax: (202) 380-4500
> E-mail: info@mgshow.org (m)
> Homepage: www.mgshow.org

Beat/Title (Additional):
Ms. Doris Abdel Messieh, Producer
Phone: (703) 251-3002
Fax: (202) 380-4500
E-mail: info@mgshow.org
Homepage: www.mgshow.org

The Judith Warner Show

A fresh perspective on pressing issues facing women today with original interviews conducted by journalist Judith Warner, author of *Perfect Madness: Motherhood in the Age of Anxiety*, a New York Times bestseller. Contact:Jennifer.Mclellan@xmradio.com; email or mail your pitch, do not call.

Life's Work with Lisa Belkin

Informal interviews with people of interest to New York Times journalist Lisa Belkin, whose *Life's Work* column focuses on the delicate, necessary, and ever-shifting balance between career, family, and personal life. Contact: Megan.Robertson@ xmradio.com; email or mail your pitch, do not call.

Broadminded

At Take Five, every night is girls' night out. There's a reason a certain premium cable series was such a hit - women know that when they get together with their girlfriends, the dishing really gets going. Join real-life friends Shari, Molly, and Christine as they let loose on sex and shopping, bad bosses and big butts, and movies and men.

Contact: Kate.Sullivan@xmradio.com; email or mail your pitch, do not call.

The Pulse
1500 Eckington Pl NE, Ste 2
Washington, DC 20002-2164

Join life coach and syndicated columnist Harriette Cole as she discusses various topics from current events to practical advice on everything from home décor to personal finance, and reviews of buzz-worthy TV shows and movies. Send your press releases, books or products to the following individual:

Ms. Harriette Cole, Host/Producer
Fax: (212) 645-3005
E-mail: askharriette@harriettecole.com
Homepage: www.harriettecole.com
Pitching tips: Cole prefers to be contacted via e-mail

Good Morning America Radio Show
147 Columbus Ave
New York, NY 10023-6503

Good Morning America Radio Show brings the best of Good Morning America in radio form. The four-hour long radio program combines news and interviews from the television version with expanded segments on stories in addition to some original content. The GMA Radio Show airs Mon-Sat from 8 a.m. to noon in all time zones.

Ms. Hilarie Barsky, Anchor
Phone: (202) 380-4000
Fax: (202) 380-4500

Preferred Order: Mail

Barsky delivers the news headlines of the day as Anchor.

Mr. Charles Gibson, Host

Phone: (212) 456-5975

Fax: (202) 380-4500

Gibson is a Host of Good Morning America and a weekly Anchor for 20/20. On Good Morning America, he covers front page events, issues and newsmakers.

Ms. Robin Roberts, Anchor

Phone: (212) 456-7809

Fax: (202) 380-4500

E-mail: robin.roberts@abc.com

Roberts is a News Anchor and Host for Good Morning America. She also serves as a correspondent for ABC News, where she contributes to other ABC programs. She also remains a contributor for ESPN.

The Sirius Satellite Radio Lineup

The Howard Stern Show

1221 Avenue Of The Americas

Fl 36

New York, NY 10020-1001

Howard's irreverent and outrageous style found a new home on Sirius radio in 2006. If your book fits his racy content, then the Howard Stern show might be on your pitching list. Entertainment program featuring news headlines, celebrity gossip and interviews and discussion that tends to focus on pop culture, sex and other adult themes. This show airs daily from 6 to 7 p.m. Send your press releases, books or products to the following people:

Mr. Benjy Bronk, Associate Producer
Phone: (212) 584-5100
Fax: (212) 584-5300
Preferred Order: Mail

Mr. Gary Dell'Abate, Producer
Phone: (212) 584-5100
Fax: (212) 584-5300

Pitching tips: Dell'Abate screens all calls and provides comic dialog for the show as Producer. On the air, he is better known as "Baba Booey." He is interested in topics such as men's issues, the entertainment industry, movies, music, current events, celebrities, and pop culture. He can be contacted by phone. Send press releases by fax.

The Business Shrink
999 Bayhill Dr, Ste 165
San Bruno, CA 94066-3069
www.allbusiness.com

Join Peter Morris for sound advice to help your business be a success. He'll not only give you advice on business strategies, he'll offer his advise on the psychology of business. This show airs daily from 3 to 4 p.m. and covers anything related to business or finance. Send your press releases, books or products to the following individual:

Mr. Peter Laufer, Executive Producer
Phone: (212) 584-5100
Fax: (212) 584-5300

Pitching Tips: Lauer oversees the entire production as Executive Producer. He is also host of National Geographic World Talk on PRI.

Coach on Call with Cheryl Richardson
PO Box 13
Newburyport, MA 01950-0013
Phone: (978) 462-2204
E-mail: radio@cherylrichardson.com
www.cherylrichardson.com

Join Cheryl Richardson for practical and no-nonsense advice on how to tackle life's many challenges. She'll bring in great life coaches to help you look at your life in a new way. This show airs daily from 5 to 6 p.m. and covers anything related to lifestyle and life issues. Send your press releases, books or products to the following individual:

Ms. Cheryl Richardson, Host/Producer
Phone: (978) 462-2204
Fax: (212) 584-5300
E-mail: radio@cherylrichardson.com
Pitching Tips: Pitch Cheryl via mail, phone or e-mail!

Whatever
1221 Avenue Of The Americas, Fl 26
New York, NY 10020-1001
E-mail: whatever@marthastewart.com

While the Ask Martha show on Sirius does not accept pitches, Martha's daughter's show will. Join Alexis Stewart and Jennifer Koppleman Hutt for a woman's kind of talk show. They'll talk about anything and everything from books to music, from personal relationships to whatever's in the news today. Alexis' mother Martha Stewart may even join the discussion. This show airs daily from noon to 2 p.m. Send your press releases, books or products to the following individuals:

Ms. Jennifer Kopplemann Hutt, Host
Phone: (212) 584-5100
Fax: (212) 584-5300
E-mail: whatever@marthastewart.com

Pitching tips: Jennifer prefers to be contacted via US Mail.

Ms. Alexis Stewart, Producer
Fax: (212) 584-5300
Pitching tips: Alexis prefers to be contacted via US Mail.

Start Ups with Joan Durand
1221 Avenue Of The Americas, Fl 36
New York, NY 10020-1001
E-mail: startups@marthastewart.com

This female focused show loves anything related to business, finance, and career. Host Joan Durand profiles women who made their dreams come true by opening up their own businesses. This show airs Saturdays from 7 to 8 p.m.

Send your press releases, books or products to the following
individual:

Ms. Joan Durand, Host/Producer
Phone: (212) 584-5100
Fax: (212) 584-5300
E-mail: startups@marthastewart.com
Pitching tips: Joan prefers to be contacted via US Mail.

Wake Up with Cosmo Radio
1221 Avenue Of The Americas, Fl 36
New York, NY 10020-1001

Join hosts Taylor Strecker and Tia Williams as they discuss
the latest celebrity and entertainment news in addition to what
stories are in the current issue of Cosmopolitan magazine.
This show airs daily from 7 to 11 a.m. in all time zones. Hosts
Taylor and Tia prefer to be contacted by mail. Send your press
releases, books or products to the following people:

Ms. Taylor Strecker, Host
Phone: (212) 584-5100
Fax: (212) 584-5300

Ms. Tia Williams, Host
Phone: (212) 584-5100
Fax: (212) 584-5300

Go to Bed with Cosmo Radio
1221 Avenue Of The Americas Fl 36
New York, NY 10020-1001

Join host Patrick Meagher as he discusses everything you want to know about the opposite sex. What better way to learn about a guy's perspective than from a man! This show airs from 7 to 11 p.m. nightly. Send your press releases, books or products to the following individual:

Mr. Patrick Meagher, Host/Producer
Phone: (212) 584-5100
Fax: (212) 584-5300

Scott Ferrall Show
1221 Avenue Of The Americas Fl 36
New York, NY 10020-1001

Join host Scott Ferrall for an entertaining show that can cover a wide span of topics. From sports to money, from travel/ adventure to women. Listen to the hilarity that ensues. This show airs Monday through Friday from 8 p.m. to 12 a.m. in all time zones. Host and Producer Scott Ferrall says he prefers to be contacted via US Mail.

Mr. Scott Ferrall, Host/Producer
Phone: (212) 584-5100
Fax: (212) 584-5300

It's All Good
1221 Avenue Of The Americas, Fl 36
New York, NY 10020-1001

Join host Claire Papin as she helps you overcome life's obstacles with practical solutions.

This show airs on Saturdays from 8 to 9 a.m.; their target demographic is listeners 18 to 34. Host and Producer Claire Papin prefers to be contacted by U.S. mail:

Ms. Claire Papin, Host/Producer
Phone: (212) 584-5100
Fax: (212) 584-5300

MEDIA TRAINING MAGIC

I always turn to the sports section first.
The sports section records people's accomplishments;
the front page nothing but man's failures.
— Earl Warren, quoted in Sports Illustrated, 22 July 1968

Whether you're doing your first interview or your 50th, you can never prepare enough for a radio or TV appearance. If you've never been media trained or coached before and you're seeking a steady stream of broadcast media, then you might want to consider this valuable component.

AME talks with producers across the U.S. regularly, and they reveal that authors are not typically the best interviewees. Usually they are timid, shy, even less than forthcoming with the information they are asked to present. What's more, some novice authors lack one big thing: enthusiasm!

Who's kidding whom? If you're not enthusiastic about your book, how can you expect the audience to give one iota of their attention to you? Passion sells. Exhibit your passion for your book or topic and your book will fly off the shelves. But, sit back, shy and somewhat indifferent, and even with the best book in world, chances are no one will be intrigued enough to buy it. This is true no matter how big the show or how great your book. Even an appearance on Oprah has been known to bring dismal sales when the author is a sleeper. You invested enough time to craft your story, and now is the time to share your zeal, joy, and message with the world. The fun is just beginning. Boast a little; be proud!

Next, you'll want to ask yourself a few questions. Your own questions that is--you know the ones you included in your media kit. Do these questions make sense? Are they still relevant today and for this audience/show? Are they fresh and interesting? Think "Tom Brokaw" if you have a topic with the potential for controversy; you can bet the interviewer is going to tap into this. Be prepared, or be prepared to be taken by surprise.

During the interview, the interviewer may or may not follow your questions. Often, they'll flex their own interviewing skills and throw you a curve-ball or a sinker. We're not talking controversy here, but just enough of a curve ball to get you off-track. Before you start any interview, make sure you know your three most important points—cold, backwards and forwards. What's your mission/Why did you write your book? These are the points that, in the absence of anything else, you want to make sure you make—the points that are designed to make the audience remember you and [hopefully] buy your book. Also, keeping your end goals in mind will help you stay on track and realign an interview that's been derailed.

Never expect that the interviewer has read your book. In fact, you'll be lucky if they even received their copy even a half hour prior to the interview. Still, it will be your job to make the interviewer look good, it's the host's show and it's your job #1 to be a good guest and make the host look like a hero for inviting you to appear on the air. Even if the host asks you a question completely unrelated to your topic, acknowledge it, answer it if you can and get them back on track without "showing them up." If you can't answer the question, say, "I don't know but I can certainly check on this and get back to you."

Finally, remember that you're going to make mistakes—everyone does, even the pros. Just smile right through them, and promise yourself to do better next time. Keep in mind when you're planning your media campaign to get your feet wet regionally first before dipping your toe into the national media pool. Why? No self-respecting producer will feature a "green" author. In other words, if you haven't paid your dues regionally or spent some serious money getting media-trained you won't attract the attention of a major show. Media draws media. The more you do, the more you'll do.

How to Prepare for a Media Interview

1) Prepare good questions: it's important to prepare good questions and expect the unexpected. Remember that the interviewer is there to get a good interview, not to "make nice" with warm and fuzzy questions. Think "Tom Brokaw," make your questions edgy (when appropriate) and even a bit controversial.

2) Q&A run through: Once you have your questions defined, run them through with an interview buddy (preferably someone who can be objective) to make sure there aren't any questions you missed or duplicate answers to questions listed.

3) People love stories: whenever possible, sprinkle anecdotes or stories into your interview - have them ready and rehearsed so you can recount them accurately

4)   What's your point? Make sure and write down five main
     points you want to cover during your interview so you
     always stay on track.

5)   Keep your interviewer happy: Make your interviewer
     look good; never, ever make them look bad or stupid
     - even if it's by accident. I guarantee you'll never get
     invited back again.

6)   Have fun! Most importantly, have fun, enjoy yourself -
     let your passion and enthusiasm for your book and topic
     shine though, people really resonate with enthusiasm and
     will often buy products based on emotion.

SECTION SIX

BUZZ, BRAGGING RIGHTS, BOOK SIGNINGS, AND MORE

*Bragging is not an attractive trait, but let's
be honest. A man who catches a big fish
doesn't go home through an alley.*
— Ann Landers

SPEAK UP!

According to most studies, people's number one fear is public speaking. Number two is death. Death is number two! Does that seem right? That means to the average person if you have to go to a funeral, you're better off in the casket than doing the eulogy.
— *Anonymous*

Authors ask me all the time: How can I get some recognition for my book? I tell them, speak up! Talk it up, whenever and wherever you can. Public speaking is powerful to not only spread the word about your book but also to build your credibility on your particular topic. The thing is, when you first become a published author, people will automatically assume you know everything about your topic (which you should). They also assume you know everything there is to know about the publishing industry as well. I'll be the first one to admit I don't know everything there is to know about the publishing world. Half the fun of it is learning something new every day. But what I do know, I can impart on others and so can you.

My first book, *The Cliffhanger*, was fiction, so the emphasis wasn't so much on the book, but on the process of publishing. Now, if you wrote a nonfiction book you can certainly speak about the topic itself at meetings, on the radio or in speeches. If your book is a historical romance, or a murder mystery, there are a number of spins your talk can take. It's not that dissimilar from pitching the media really. The thing is, in this instance, you're pitching for a speaking engagement. Most of the time, you'll be speaking for free. But don't let that discourage you because there's a little thing called "back of the room sales" that can make it all worthwhile for you Most speaking engagements will allow you to sell your book, and gain valuable speaking experience at the same time.

If the thought of getting up in front of a crowd of people makes you more nervous than a turkey the week before Thanksgiving, know that if you can overcome your fear, public speaking is a powerful tool to get the word out about you and your book. Most people think that when they sign up to speak publicly they have to develop a persona or gimmick. I say, be yourself. Script what you're going to say, then toss the script and work from 3 x 5 cards so you'll sound more natural and not just a talking head. Go to a Toastmaster's class a few times and get some pointers from the pros. I did this once and was amazed at how many times I said "uh". Uh, get the picture? There are many, many topics you can speak on and even more places to do just that. Your local Chamber of Commerce is always looking for speakers. How about an organization relating to your topic? There are hundreds of them out there. Check your city's upcoming events calendar. If you pick an event related to your topic with a date that's eight to 12 months out, they are probably still in need of speakers and there might be a spot open with your name on it.

If you're looking for events to speak at, why not trade shows? Most of them have an educational arm you might be able to participate in. Cruise on over to www.tsnn.com for a complete listing of trade shows both nationally and internationally.

Interested in adding to your speaking engagements? How about libraries? Whether local or while you're away, libraries across the country are always in the market for a good program they can present to their patrons. Head on over to the American Library Association at www.ala.org/publicprograms/authors@ yourlibrary. You can even submit your information so librarians can find out about you. Just click on the "Submission Form for Publishers" and list yourself.

BUILDING THE BUZZ

Success seems to be largely a matter of
hanging on after others have let go.
— *William Feather*

About a year before they opened, I began hearing that Krispy Kreme had selected our fine city to open up its first shop in the area. None of us living in Southern California had ever eaten one of their donuts. Except maybe those lucky enough to travel back east where these shops are everywhere. But from what I heard, they were amazing. When the Krispy Kreme shop finally opened in my area, you could expect to wait nearly two hours for your own Krispy Kreme goodie. Well, my girlfriends and I simply could no longer resist. So we stood among hundreds of others waiting patiently for our first taste of a real Krispy Kreme donut. Television cameras were everywhere, radio stations were broadcasting from their rooftops, and it was amazing. Finally, we had our box. Sitting on a bench we each tried one, and guess what? They were donuts. Okay, they were good. But still, they were donuts. All of this commotion, and all over a donut. Amazing when you think about it, isn't it? That's buzz. It doesn't matter if it's a cure for cancer or a new donut shop. A buzz is a buzz in whatever form. It drives the public's attention. The same can be said for movies, techie gadgets, t-shirt sheets, even pink

Ugg boots. Think about the books you've bought based on buzz alone. A good buzz will generate media interest and thus public interest and even after it's launched, it can survive for a long time just on buzz alone.

I spoke to a publisher who told me once that often, most literary houses won't even consider a manuscript if it arrives "sans" buzz. So how do you go about creating a buzz on something that hasn't even hit the streets yet? Well, you could do what Richard Paul Evans, the author of *The Christmas Box*, did. Even though it wasn't published traditionally, he still wanted people to read his book. So he printed off copies, had them bound at his local copy shop and gave them away to everyone he knew. The book was so good that eventually, it started a buzz. He had people calling him he didn't even know asking for a copy of his book. He sold many thousands of copies in the Salt Lake City area alone. Needless to say, he did eventually get it published. And by the time it arrived at the publisher it was loaded with buzz. So much so that the major publishers became interested in the book and dozens of them participated in a two-day auction. Simon & Schuster came out the winner. They only had to pay Evans a $4.2 million advance. The book has sold more than 7,000,000 copies in 17 different languages.

That's the beauty of self-publishing. You can publish your book, get it out there and start creating such an interest about it that the buzz naturally follows. Eventually, the media will pick up on this and then, if you're lucky, a publisher will stand up and take notice. Now, this, of course, is no guarantee that you'll get picked up traditionally. But more often than not, if a publisher sees that you've got something big, they're going to want a part of it.

Start marketing your book early. There are a variety of things you can start doing prior to your book being available for purchase. You could, for example, start an e-mail newsletter (more on that later), or submit articles to a variety of trade magazines. If you're having postcards printed, get them printed early as well as your bookmarks. But the most important thing here is that you have a place for people to go once you've gotten them interested in your book or topic. Get your Web site up and running and make sure people can sign up for either a mailing list, e-mail newsletter or let them make an advance purchase of your book. If you're taking advance purchases, offer your readers a substantial discount as an incentive to buy early.

Some authors will begin generating buzz by planning events surrounding the release of their book; some will even plan them well in advance of the release, as far out as three months. Keep in mind that if you can pull this off, great! But sometimes you can't go back to the media-well twice, meaning that if your local media has covered this once, they might not do it again. If you're planning to do a lot of advance promotion it will be important to keep the story fresh. Change the topic or event so the idea doesn't get stale.

Another good, but somewhat time consuming way to start people talking about your book is to initiate an online discussion about it. Again, this works best if it's a non-fiction genre or hot topic. Places like talkcity.com or about.com host hundreds of topic discussions. Begin by creating your own community or starting your own topic. You can begin to generate interest about your book. Most places will offer these services for free. Yahoo!Groups for example is a great place to start an online discussion group and the best part of this is that they offer their service for free. You can invite people to join or often what I'll do is get a sign-up sheet going at a book signing and invite those people to join this discussion group. It's amazing how quickly it will grow. One person tells another and so on. Keep your e-mail discussion groups lively and interesting, give them a reason to become a member and stay a member.

If you want to do a targeted e-mail campaign, start collecting names from your Web site. Have people sign up for your e-mail newsletter or an announcement mailing list. Sometimes you can even purchase a list to start a target e-mail campaign, direct sales or newsletter blurbs.

BRAGGING RIGHTS

When ideas fail, words come in very handy.
— Goethe

Like becoming a new parent or grandparent, you too have bragging rights. So when someone asks you what you do, what exactly do you tell them? Do you say: "I like to write." Or do you proudly tout the fact that you're a published author? People are very impressed with those of us who are published. They love hearing our stories and asking us what our book is about. But before you launch into an entire dialog about your book, topic, and characters, remember your elevator pitch. Keep your responses short, and intriguing. Remember that while most people will simply want to know if you've been on Oprah, you might inspire someone else to finish their book or you could also be speaking to someone who could directly benefit from your work.

So now, what are you going to tell people when they ask what you do? What one line can you come up with that will intrigue them and get them to ask more, and possibly, even buy your book. Think about it. Did you perhaps write a story about a girl who gets herself out of an abusive relationship? How about telling people you are an expert on women who get themselves into and out of abusive relationship?" No doubt you did a mountain of research for your book so you probably know what you're talking about. And if you're doing the talk circuit thing, you're probably knee deep in statistics, and crisis centers.

When you reach out to people like this, it's not always about you. Sure, it starts out that way. But when you tell someone you're the expert on a particular topic, I guarantee you they'll know someone who could benefit or know someone who knows someone. You might even be in a position to help someone who's lost all hope, and wouldn't that be great? It doesn't always have to be the kind of assistance that will get you the Medal of Honor or a float in the Rose Parade. It could be something as simple as empowering another human being to live their dream and get that book published. Who knows, while you're standing in line at the post office telling the person in front of you that you're a published author, you could be talking to your next customer or someone who could land you a lucrative bulk sale deal. Don't just rely on a press release to spread your message. Some of the most successful authors talk about their work to anyone who will listen. In fact, I'm not ashamed to say that I'm one of those chatty authors. Sure, it's bragging. But after persisting through enough rejection letters to wallpaper my house, I think I've earned it.

BOOK SIGNINGS

A signature always reveals a man's character —
and sometimes even his name.
— Evan Esar

So what do you do when you have a book signing and no one shows up? Sure, that may sound like the beginning of a great joke, but for many of us, it's our worst nightmare.

One of the scariest moments in my life was my first book signing. Even more frightening than having my first signing was the fact that I was doing it out of town and wouldn't have my support group of friends to stop by and play the role of excited fans. But I had done everything by the book so to speak. First, I sent some advance copies of the book to the storeowner, I mailed him the book cover posters, I made up bag stuffers and sent the proper press releases to local media. To my chagrin when I arrived there, the box containing my marketing materials was still sealed. Not one poster was out, not one bag stuffer had been used. Worst of all, it poured rain that day. So there I sat, my dreams of crowds lining up outside the little shop vanishing with each passing second. When one person did show up, I nearly jumped out of my chair to embrace them. Thankfully, I managed to contain myself. About an hour after the book signing started, I noticed several people in the store, none of them paying attention to me. So, I got up and began to walk around the store. I carried my book with me and each time I came across someone perusing romance, I would engage them in conversation. Often, I would hand them a copy of my book and tell them I was in there for a book signing. The mere act of holding my book in their hand induced ownership and often, a sale would follow. But it wasn't so much about the sale. In the end it was about selling myself. It was about becoming a memorable author. If the person I was speaking to wasn't interested in romance, perhaps they had a friend who was. After that first signing, I realized that a successful book signing isn't having people lined up out the door, although if that were to happen, I'd be in book signing heaven! It's about getting your books in the store, having a place to sit and maybe, if you're lucky, having one person show up. That first book signing really helped to put this into perspective for me.

Doing an Event?

The Event Guide www.eventguide.com is great for finding out what's going on in a city you may be doing an event in or trying to position yourself on an already planned event!

The Buddy System

Some authors like to have another person there signing with them so they don't have to sit there looking lost and lonely. I've done it both ways and they each have their merits. First of all, the buddy system will probably bring in more people since you are essentially doubling your publicizing efforts (or at least you should be). You can turn a simple book signing into an event. One of you can be having a book discussion or workshop, while the other author is signing. It's a great way to draw a crowd and keep a crowd. Also, often it's easier to get publicity when there's more than one author present. Unless, of course, you're Nora Roberts, in which case you can probably ignore the buddy system altogether. This type of book signing works well for unknown authors if you have a specific program or want to have a book signing that lasts all day.

Book Fairs

If you're targeting book fairs here's a great link to get your started: http://www.literarysource.com/fairsandfestivals.htm

No Sitting On The Job

As I mentioned previously, don't just sit there and smile. Get up, move around and engage people in conversation. Would you believe I've been told that some shoppers are actually intimidated to just walk up and talk to an author? But, if you speak to them first you're breaking the ice and maybe, making a sale. Take your focus off of yourself and your stack of books and put it on the people in the store. As with anything in marketing, you're really selling yourself and trying to focus on people in the process. Try getting up from your chair to greet people as they enter the store. I usually have a small flyer made up with the cover of my book, a blurb about it and I tell people I'm signing books today. Smile and talk to them and hand them a book. Begin to tell them about your novel. Get them excited about it—let your passion shine through. Passion is a very contagious thing. People want to feel that same passion and folks love being around passionate people.

Go See What the Competition is Doing

Have you ever visited someone else's book signing? I did once and I felt like everyone there knew what I was up to. I wanted to see what it was about, to see what other authors did. Some of your best ideas or taboos will come from watching other people. I remember the first one I went to, I entered the store and there she was, the smiling author, pen ready and a stack of books looming over the table. I wondered if I were just a customer that happened into the store, what would make me walk up to her unless my specific purpose had been to attend this signing? Then, I wondered what I could do to draw that traffic. Face it, no matter how much publicizing you do, unless you've got a spot on *Good Morning America* to talk up your signing, most of your foot traffic will probably just be shoppers. If you're really lucky you'll see some frantic people in search of last minute gifts; autographed books make great presents!

If you want to pick up tips from the pros, you might try visiting a celebrity signing or two. Check out the Publisher's Weekly Web site at www.publishersweekly.com for a listing of upcoming signings. The book section of your local newspaper is another great resource. Also, if you're going on the road for any reason, check out these sites and see if there's an event you can attend while you're away.

Be Unique!

If your book involves anything that you can tie in with a theme or a prop, all the better. I went to a book signing for an author who specialized in period romance. This particular novel was set during the 1600's and she dressed in a gown fitting to the time. She also had a castle backdrop that a neighbor painted for her. Her neighbor was an aspiring artist, so not only was she doing the author a favor but the neighbor got to showcase her work as well. People really love this kind of a thing. I mean anyone can sit at a table and smile, but sitting there in a corset for four hours takes real passion. So give some thought to what you can do to tie in a theme or prop into your signing. You don't necessarily have to show up in costume, but try to do what you can to set yourself apart from the rest. The important thing here is that while it's good to learn from the competition, you don't necessarily want to be exactly like them, either.

Stuff To Do Before Your Book Signing

- See if you can get a copy of the store's media list. More than likely the bookstore will send out press releases but it's important for you to do the same. Not only will you be able to target the same people twice, but the store manager will also know that you are actively involved in promoting your event.

- Send a confirmation of your signing to the bookstore. It will make you look professional and show the store manager that you are a professional and that you take your book signings very seriously. A sample of the form I use follows this chapter.

- Start tapping into that media list you've been creating and begin contacting local media to promote your event.

- Post your book signing information on the Author Appearances section of your Web site. Get invitations made up or make them yourself and send everyone on your contact list an invitation to your signing.

- If you haven't already done so, get those bookmarks and postcards printed up. Don't forget to include the ISBN of your book, include a few review blurbs if you have them. Get the cover of your book enlarged to poster size. Then, get it laminated and mounted. I had three of them printed up. I will usually drop one or two off at the store prior to the event so they can set them out and I'll bring the third one with me that day. Prop a sign up on an easel by the front door where you will be standing and greeting people. If you have the time and the budget, get a set of colorful pens made up with the title of the book and author's name imprinted on it then when you sign the book, give the reader the pen. It's another great way to spread the word about your book!

- Get signs made that say: "Book Signing Today" or "Author Appearance;" both of these will help to draw crowds to your table.

Things To Bring To Your Book Signing

- Bookmarks – I try to hand these out like crazy. Sometimes I'll even hand them out with the flyer when people enter the store. I've even autographed one or two when people hesitate to buy a book. More often than not, they return at a later time to buy a copy just because I gave them a bookmark.

- Postcards – bring postcards with your book cover on them. I always say you can never have too many marketing materials.

- Chocolate – I like to fill an attractive jar with Hershey's kisses or some other small chocolate. Food attracts people and may even keep them lingering a bit longer.

- Guest book – I always have people sign in at the event. If they give you their e-mail address, inquire as to whether you can add them to your mailing list. This is a great way to build a "fan club" and continue spreading the word about your book as well as future novels. If you don't feel comfortable with a guest book, try putting together a free drawing. Tell them they don't have to be present to win. People hate that; I know I do. I mean who wants to stick around a book signing for four hours? Well, okay, except for the author. You should do what you can to keep a log of people that purchased your book. It's a great way to build your mailing list and customer base.

- Make up a small flyer to hand to people who enter the store. They may not even know about your signing but you'll be sure to tell them. Keep in mind that heavy promotion of your book signing does not just benefit you, it also benefits the store and sends a strong message that you know how to move your books.

- Your favorite pen.

During Your Signing

• Don't sit down unless you have to.

• Smile, talk and most of all have fun! This is no time to be shy.

• If no one shows up, remember, that's okay. It has happened to all of us at one time or another.

• Get people to enter your contest or sign your guest book.

• Tell the store manager that you'd like to sign the remaining books before you leave the store and see if they have "Autographed by Author" stickers for them. If they don't, you might want to think about ordering some from the American Booksellers Association (www.bookWeb.org). You can get these and a variety of other book stickers for $5 a roll. These stickers will really help to move your book.

• Don't feel confined to stay just a few hours. Stay as long as there is an interest in the book. Once, I booked a signing for two hours; I ended up staying for five.

What To Do After Your Book Signing

Send a thank you note to the person in charge of coordinating your signing. Don't send an e-mail. Send a handwritten note. It will go a lot further!

A Few Final Notes on Book Signings

Be cautious of pay periods when scheduling a date for your signing. For example, I will always try to schedule mine around the 15th or 30th of the month. I live in a Navy town and since they never fail to get paid on those dates, it really helps to boost my sales. Also, check to see if the store has a newsletter. If it does, offer to write a short article on your book or discussion topic that will draw more attention to your signing. Keep the article interesting and helpful without giving away everything you plan to share with your guests. Or, if your book is fiction, share an interesting excerpt from it. Sometimes bookstore newsletters are printed by their corporate offices but generally they print them in-house and are always in need of "filler" items.

Also, contact your local TV stations and speak to the producer. Call the day before (if your signing is on Sunday call them on Friday) and let him know you've sent a press release regarding your signing (you have, haven't you?). If they need a 60-second filler, you can offer their viewers some helpful tips on XYZ. Or, if your book is fiction, play up the "local author makes big" angle. Local stations love that. Speaking of media, if you can get yourself booked on a radio show the day before or preferably the morning of your signing, you'll really help to boost interest. If you get some on-air time, consider giving away a few of your books during the show. And remember to tie your book and event into something topical and relevant!

Check the book section of your local newspaper. Many times they will announce author events. If they do, you want to make sure yours is included! Be sure to send them a notice of your event at least a month out.

And finally, send a quick confirmation letter when you do get a book signing. It shows your professionalism and lets the store know you're serious about this. Here's a sample of how one should look. Feel free to vary these depending on your book and the store.

XYZ Bookstore
123 Elm Street
San Diego, CA 92142

Dear XYZ:

This letter is to confirm that Penny C. Sansevieri will be doing a signing on November 25, 2005 from 10 a.m. to 3 p.m. at the following address:

XYZ Bookstore
123 Elm Street
San Diego, CA 92142

(List the bookstore name and address again in case one store books signings for all of their other locations).

The book featured will be: *From Book to Bestseller*. This book can be ordered in advance from the publisher: Fantastic Publishing (877) 555-4737 (always list the 800 number for ordering). We suggest ordering a quantity of 20 books for this event.

Thank you again for booking this event. I know it will be a success. I will be contacting local media in the area to notify them of this event and will keep you posted on any media coverage scheduled. If there are any changes to this event or if it needs to be rescheduled, please contact my office immediately at (858) 560-0121.

Sincerely,

Penny C. Sansevieri

Want to know who's selling your book? Check out <u>www. bookhq.com</u>.

Is Your Book a Virgin?

Virgin, the mega music store is now looking to branch out into books, adding them to about 20 locations in the U.S. in part to help the sagging music business. The New York Time's Square store opened their book section in September of 2005. Other stores will follow throughout 2006 and 2007. This might be a great time to inquire about an in-store event especially if your book has a hip-music appeal or some sort of tie-in.

BOOK TOURS

Writing and travel broaden your bottom if
not your mind and I like to write standing up.
— Ernest Hemingway

A typical book tour can cost a traditional publisher upwards of $60,000 and send an author into a whirlwind of appearances, ribbon cutting ceremonies and other celebrity-like events. Book tours, while a great idea, don't have to cost you your entire marketing budget and then some. If you're funding your own campaign, a book tour should be carefully planned to last no more than a few days or a week at the very most. If you can step away from your life for longer than that, great. But more often than not, it's not feasible to be gone from your full-time activities for two to three months.

If you have a book and are trying to figure out where you should target your book signing, here are a few things to consider. First of all, it's great if you can visit your hometown and do a trek through some of the neighboring cities. People love it when one of their own has become "famous" and you'll soon begin to realize that once you've gotten published, people will immediately begin to believe that you're having lunch with the likes of Steven Spielberg and Diane Sawyer. So, I say go with it. No, don't lie about who you're dining with these days, but ride the wave of fame as long as it will carry you. Contact your local Chamber of Commerce, Kiwanis and Lion's Club organizations. They're always looking for speakers. Get in touch with all of the bookstores in the area as well as libraries and schools. Let everyone know you're coming to town, I guarantee they will want to jump on the author tour bandwagon. Another option for your book tour is the location where your story takes place. In *The Cliffhanger*, my love story happened in Newport, Oregon, in a fictional hotel called The Cliffhanger. It was a natural location for my first book tour. For me, after the rigors of trying to get my book published, it was like a dream come true. I was headed up to Oregon to speak at a Chamber of Commerce luncheon in the town of Newport where *The Cliffhanger* took place. I had even managed to schedule a few book signings and a radio interview. When one store couldn't schedule me for a signing, I offered to come in and sign their stock of books anyway (remember that "Autographed by Author" sticker).

An Alternative to Touring the Country

Tour the Net instead. Doing an author tour on the net can be a much better and less expensive way to do a tour than flying around the country.

Interested in our Virtual Author Tour™? E-mail us at <u>info@ amarketingexpert.com</u>

Don't feel pressured to do an author tour. Certainly, if you can afford them they're a great way to get the word out about your books as long as they are appropriate to your market. If you need to cut expensive travel costs, do what Bobbie Christensen does on her trips. She tours in her RV and stays in KOA campgrounds for $20 a night. Sure, it might not be the most glamorous way to do your first tour, but you could probably visit more spots this way. Whatever you decide to do, author tours can be great but exhausting. Once you've done your first book signing you'll understand what I mean. An afternoon in the store, smiling and talking and being a perfect host or hostess, really takes it out of you. Then take that and times it by 50 and you've got a general idea of how tired you're going to be.

Promotional Tip

Going on the road? Don't forget to list yourself with "Authors on the Highway" at www.bookwire.com/bookwire/ netread/index.html. This site is viewed by both the general public as well as industry professionals.

Other places to add your event listing are:

www.publishersweekly.com/index asp?layout=authorsmain

www.netread.com

www.writerswrite.com/events

Timing is everything

Most large publishing houses don't tour authors during the summer months (July and August). So if you want to book a tour, consider doing it then. A good advantage to this is that you can draw on the tourist traffic as well. Especially if you have a fiction book set in the town you're visiting.

Booksale Finder!

If you're looking for book fairs, book events, or conferences, check out Booksale Finder at: Booksale Finder http://www. booksalefinder.com/ - just plug in the location you're looking for and the site will pull up a complete list of events in the area.

SECTION EIGHT

A FEW FINAL MARKETING STRATEGIES

The possession of knowledge does not kill the sense of wonder and mystery. There is always more mystery.
— Anaïs Nin

NETWORKING GOLD

*More business decisions occur over lunch and dinner than at
any other time, yet no MBA courses are given on the subject.*
— *Peter Drucker*

Whether you're trying to find an editor for your book,
or a producer to pitch your story to, sometimes it's all about
networking. If you still have 999 of the 1,000 business cards
you ordered, you're not getting out there enough. It's time
to step out from behind that computer and strike networking
gold.

One of the first laws of networking is that you want to
get to know the people you're networking with. If you're at
a writer's conference or networking luncheon, don't just pass
out business cards, take the time to get to know people. When
you meet industry partners, jot down a few notes on the back of
their business cards so you don't lose this potentially valuable
information.

When you're building your network, be generous with your
help and information. The people you're networking with will
remember and appreciate your generosity. Next, you'll want
to stay on their radar screen. If I don't regularly dialog with a
particular contact, I try to send them a note or set up a lunch at
least once every six months (more when I can). When you're

staying in touch with people, let them know if you're offering a new service or product and always remember to send thank you notes whenever you get a referral from them.

If your objective is to join some networking groups, remember that these are not all created equal. Some groups and events are better than others and some are just straight out time wasters. When you first start pursuing networking events, you'll find that many are just "luncheons," meaning that a few entrepreneurs get together and hash out their difficulties/ideas/ challenges over lunch. If this is what you're after, great! But more than likely you'll want to attend events that can sell you books, get you new business or a combination of both. Keep in mind also that some networking events cost money to join, so weigh the benefits of membership before you plunk down some cash. The better organizations don't always need to cost a lot, often you can find networking organizations that only charge a small fee at the door to cover room expenses, etc.

The next thing you'll want to look at when attending a networking meeting is supply and demand. If you're promoting your business and looking for leads, you probably won't want to go to a meeting where there are a number of people doing the same thing you are. Unless it's an association (those are great too) you'll want to look for meetings that have a good balance in attendees.

Are you ready to network?

Before you head off to your first meeting, be sure you have your networking checklist in order. This checklist might vary from meeting to meeting depending on the audience and your own changing goals and objectives.

What benefits can I bring to the people attending this event?

Am I prepared with my quick "about me" speech for introductions.

What are at least three goals I'd like to achieve by attending this meeting?

Who is hosting this networking meeting? (you'll want to be sure and thank them for their hard work)

What materials (besides business cards) do I need to bring with me to the meeting?

The other obvious choice for writers is writer's conferences. But much like networking meetings, they are not all created equal. Once you determine that you want to attend a conference, start "shopping" for the right one to attend. You'll need to find a conference that fits your writing needs right now. For example, if you're still in the throes of getting into the craft of writing, perhaps a writing retreat is more suited to your needs. If you've already written a book and are deciding what to do with it, then a more advanced conference will work better for you. In either case, peruse their Web sites carefully. Recommendations are great but remember, attending the wrong conference can be a waste of your time and money. Spend both of these commodities wisely!

Whether you're meeting a producer for coffee, attending a networking event or going to your first writer's conference there are a few tips that you'll want to keep in mind. First, whenever you collect business cards, take a few minutes to jot down some notes on the back before proceeding onto your next prospect. You can note some of the discussion you had or what your follow-up action might be. Next, you'll want to follow up while the contact is still fresh. Especially if you're at a writer's conference or some other big event where there's a lot of networking.

There's nothing like networking to build your business or sell books, but remember that much like marketing, networking is all about relationships. Building them, supporting them, and, ultimately, benefiting from them. Like anything, becoming a good networker takes time and effort, but when done correctly, it's worth all the work you put into it because you never know, networking gold today might mean a spot on Oprah tomorrow.

Sometimes attending a networking meeting can be a bit intimidating, especially when you're new to the group. When that happens try to network with people you know or have similar interests or hobbies. Many times a common ground can be a great ice breaker!

THE CREDIBILITY FACTOR

Either write something worth reading
or do something worth writing about.
— *Ben Franklin*

In recent years, media relations has changed drastically. The funny, cute and innovative press kits authors and publicists used to send have been replaced with kits that focus in on one major issue: credibility. In a world of corporate scandals, Martha Stewart, and questionable journalism, what you see isn't always what you get. If you've been having a hard time getting PR of late, perhaps it has nothing to do with your story. Now, I'm not suggesting that your credibility is in question, but maybe you haven't spent enough time emphasizing it in your pitch and press kit. More often, I find that authors who represent themselves can sometimes be their own worst enemies. Not wanting to toot their own horns, they leave it up to the reporter or editor to sift through their credentials to determine whether or not they are viable candidates for interviews. As a savvy PR person, you shouldn't leave this up to them. You should take control of your own credibility factor.

Credibility Tip

If you're wondering how "credible" you are know this: much of the media searches for their experts online. If your online presence is lacking, you might want to garner some media exposure in the way of blogs, online reviews, and online article syndication (for more on these topics, see Striking Internet Gold)

It's not only the media who are seeking credibility for their guests, but viewers and customers have come to question what they used to take for granted. So, what does this mean for you? Well, take a look at the book you've written; if you haven't done everything you can to position yourself as an expert and hype your credentials, you should look at doing this as soon as possible. Conversely, if you have written your book through experience and don't necessarily have the credentials it takes to be authoritative, then maybe you need to look at having someone coauthor the book with you. Or, perhaps you can get someone in the field to write a foreword for the book.

Credibility does, however, come in a variety of forms. If you're looking to enhance or build on your credibility, there are some distinct ways you can do that. First, media exposure will help lend itself to credibility among your potential customers. Being on TV or radio will help to enhance your exposure and credibility with your audience. Second, you can also help enhance your credibility through industry involvement. Speak at events as opportunities present themselves, or submit articles to these niche publications. Credibility and expert status will often go hand in hand, so keep in mind that anything you do to leverage your status as an expert will also lend itself to enhancing your credibility as well.

These days, credibility is more important than ever. Fewer and fewer authors can just "get by" with limited exposure and minimal credibility. Don't shortchange yourself on interviews by minimizing your background and knowledge; include any and all relevant credentials. The inclusion of these credentials might make all the difference to the success of your book!

BOOK A RE-LAUNCH!

There is no pleasure in the world like
writing well and going fast.
— Tennessee Williams

Marketing a book can often be a daunting task, but if your campaign has stalled, maybe it's time for a re- launch. Re-launching your book can often be a great way to help invigorate your efforts and reignite a stalled book. But there are certain components that need to be in place to make a re-launch successful. First, you'll need to have a reason to re-launch (besides a stalled campaign). Some of the things that might make your book a good candidate for a re- launch are:

New information: If your topic warrants an update, now might be a time to consider it. There's nothing worse than selling a book with outdated information. It doesn't speak well of you or your product!

Reviews: If you're finally getting your reviews back and they are stellar, this might be another reason to consider a re-launch, especially if you can combine this with some topic updates. It can breathe new life into your book and marketing campaign.

Endorsements: If you've been going after celebrity endorsements or endorsements of any kind and they are finally coming back to you, then this could be another reason to consider a re-launch of your book.

Foreword: If the foreword you were so eager for came through after the book was printed, or if you've finally identified the perfect person to write a foreword, this might be another reason for a re- launch, especially if the foreword helps leverage your credibility.

Many times I'll teach classes with students who tell me "if only I had known." Don't let this new information discourage you. If you should decide to re-launch your book, you can always utilize all these savvy marketing ideas for your new campaign. A former client of mine, Mindy Gibbins-Klein, recently re-launched her book, "A Dance in the Desert." While the book was outstanding, Mindy felt that it was languishing a bit and needed a new surge. Turns out Mindy was right: Within days of the re-release and her newly designed campaign, the book shot up the UK Amazon rankings to within the 5,000 range. Keep in mind that a re-launch works best when several of the above components are in place. But this might also be a good time to consider updating your cover, rewriting your back copy, or adding or deleting segments of your book. If you're going to go through the effort of a re-launch, you'll want to give all of your readers a reason to buy, even those who purchased your first edition. Then, when the changes are done, add "Revised Updated Edition" to the cover. This will tell your potential customer that it's a fresh edition, with new information, and they have to look no further for it than your book.

HOW TO LAND YOUR BOOK ON A BESTSELLER LIST!

Thank your readers and the critics
who praise you, and then ignore them.

Write for the most intelligent, wittiest,
wisest audience in the universe:

Write to please yourself.
— Harlan Ellison

Next to getting on Oprah, I'd have to say that the biggest request I get from authors is their desire to be on the New York Times bestseller list. Is this an impossible goal? No, but depending on your book, it might not be the right target for you. Why? Because the New York Times bestseller list is not based on sales figures but what booksellers feel is selling and popular, which is why this particular bestseller list has often been referred to as a popularity contest. The key to targeting a bestseller list and to gaining bestseller status for your book is to first understand how these lists work.

First, let's take a peek at the much-publicized Amazon. com bestseller program. Lots of authors are doing this, but is this a goal that's right for you? Before we determine that, let's take a closer look at how these programs work. First and foremost, getting to the top of the Amazon.com bestseller list overall is a very tough target to hit. Given the 4 million titles Amazon.com stocks, surging your book up these ranks would require Herculean sales. But what most authors don't know is that you can surge your book into bestseller status without being a bestseller overall. Let me explain. Amazon divides their books into categories or lists. They have regional lists and lists within a particular category - what this means is that you might be ranked at 10,000 overall, but ranked 500 within your category.

When my book, The Cliffhanger, became an Amazon. com bestseller as described in an earlier chapter,, it did this by becoming the bestselling book within a region, in this case San Diego. Now the key factor to remember is that you might gain bestseller status within your category but it might not mean that much to you in the way of sales. What I mean is this: If your category is comprised of let's say five other books, then all you have to do is sell five books to get to the #1 spot. Now, most categories will probably have more books in them but you get the idea. The more obscure your topic, the less likely you are to have competition. The flipside to this is having the cache of being an Amazon.com bestselling author, regardless of the amount of books you had to sell to get there – although ideally it's thousands, this isn't always the case. So before plunking down good money to be a part of a campaign like this understand that it's really just a numbers game and it might not mean that sales always tilt in your favor.

So how can you spike Amazon and force your book up the ranks? Simple. Target a large group of readers and give them a short window within which to buy your book, ideally 24 hours. Then offer the readers so many amazing bonuses they'd be nuts to buy your book outside of this offer. The tricky part will be in getting the audience. Many authors who have done this will get mailings lists, or borrow lists and ask e-mail marketers with announcement lists or e-zines to partner with them, thereby tapping into a larger group of people and expanding their reach. So, how large an audience will you need to target? Well, that depends on how many other fish there are in your pool. If you're in a category that's packed, let's say diet, then you're probably looking at an e-mail blast to a half-million people, if it's in a more obscure category you might be able to get away with 50,000 or so. The key is knowing your category and knowing what it will take to surge the list. By focusing on your category this does not mean that you can't alter your overall standings. An e-mail blast of this size will probably move you up in the overall rankings and, in some cases, get you into the coveted Amazon top 10 overall standings.

So if Amazon isn't your thing, how can you get onto other bestseller lists? Well, let's break them down. We've already determined that the New York Times list is based on feedback from bookstores and not sales figures; The Wall Street Journal operates in much the same way. Both papers poll approximately 3,000 stores each. This is great if your book has excellent bookstore presence, but if you're a small publisher or a print-on-demand author, this probably isn't the case and as most of us know, even if you're traditionally published your book may not see the inside of a bookstore.. USA Today, however, does base their list on sales figures and is probably the most accurate of all the national lists. There are also regional bestseller lists as well as trade or specialty lists. Many times books can surge in regions or categories (not that dissimilar from the Amazon rankings) and never peak on a national list.

The key to getting a bestseller is to understand the market for your book, your competition and most certainly, your book's availability. In order to key in on one of the prestigious bestseller lists like the New York Times or The Wall Street Journal, your book obviously has to have a large bookstore presence and be selling well. If you have one but not the other, you probably won't be seeing your title on either of these lists. If your book has a heavy regional presence, and your local newspaper has a focused bestseller list for just your region, then taking a shot at that list might work.

The challenge for most of these lists is book availability. If no one can get your book, there's zero hope of a bestseller mention, and the problem with most authors aspiring to become bestsellers is that they don't realize how significant distribution can be. I have personally known a few sure-thing celebrity titles that have sold next to nothing because they weren't in active distribution channels. And this is particularly true for the print-on-demand author and small press author.

So if your goal is bestseller status, be reasonable about the target you go after. Shooting for a target that, even on the best of days, would elude you will do nothing but steal from the moment of your campaign. Targeting a list that you have the ability to crack is an attainable goal and one (with the right promotion) you might just be able to hit.

PUBLICITY FROM THIRTY-THOUSAND FEET

I'm not a very good writer, but I'm an excellent rewriter.
— James Michener

We all know that marketing a book is a process. But sometimes the process takes longer than we'd anticipated. That's why it's nice every now and again to hop aboard the publicity jet and get a look-see at what you've been doing from the 30,000 foot level. Why? Well, first off this birds-eye view will reveal to you areas you might be overlooking or other options for marketing you hadn't considered.

To accomplish this birds-eye view you'll want to get yourself a big white board, or something else big enough to chart your flight plan on. Then, once you've gotten that, start charting the course you've taken so far. Don't leave a single thing out; it doesn't matter what it is. What you want to end up with is a serious list of everything you've done from the time you held your first proof book in your hands.

One of the things this type of a project will do is give you a new perspective on what you're doing. It will show you areas that you've possibly been spending too much time on or potential holes in your campaign. Sketching out your marketing campaign will also give you a chance to see what's been leveraging you results and what hasn't. Keep in mind that some things like bulk sales and national media might take longer than other items so you'll want to keep putting forth effort towards those long- term goals. But let's say you've been spending tons of time doing radio but nothing really seems to be happening in that area. You then look over to your speaking engagement section and realize you haven't done a lot with that recently. Perhaps it's time to pull back on radio and start pushing speaking events.

Once you've spent a good long time in this birds-eye view mode, start developing a to-do list of items or add to an existing list to help reinvigorate your campaign. One of the many things you'll learn from doing this 30,000 foot perspective is that we often become myopic in our campaigns, focusing too hard in one area and not hard enough in another. Stepping back from your work will allow you the breathing room you need to regroup and reset your goals. Then you can focus in on particular areas or tasks that might need a boost.

It's been said that a plane flying from Hawaii to Los Angeles is always off by three percent. If left to fly without any adjustments to the course, however slight, the plane would land up in Seattle instead (a difference of almost 1,200 miles!). But through corrections and readjustments the pilot eventually reaches his destination. As you pilot your own campaign, remember: don't leave your marketing on autopilot. Realign, readjust, and refocus and eventually you too will reach your destination, wherever that might be.

What's a Platform?

You've probably heard it a million times: "you must have a platform." But what exactly is a platform? Well, many times it's the difference between making a book sale and sending a potential customer to buy someone else's book instead. If you envision a platform as something you stand on, then the components that elevate you can be any one (or all of) the following:

Your business

The size of your audience or your following The strength of your credentials or expertise in a field Media training or media experience

Who do you know or who knows you i.e. can you get well-respected people in your industry to endorse or review your book?

Your speaking career

Any products you've developed related to your topic/book Any articles you've published on your particular topic

Whether fiction or non-fiction, having a platform can be crucial to furthering your career as a writer and if your ultimate goal is to ink a deal with a corporate publisher, then a platform isn't just crucial, it's mandatory. If you haven't spent a lot of time creating your platform then maybe you should

MAKING THE MOST OF AMAZON.COM

*There are two kinds of people, those who do the work
and those who take the credit. Try to be in the first group;
there is less competition there.*
— *Indira Gandhi*

Besides being a great place to shop, Amazon also offers considerable marketing opportunities for anyone willing to take the time to explore them. Here are just a few you might want to consider. Keep in mind that Amazon's site is not static, meaning that they are in a constant state of change. If any of these items aren't available on the site, keep checking back because Amazon will often shuffle features to gauge their individual popularity.

Tell Amazon Who You Are

One of the first things you'll want to do is register yourself on Amazon. Once you do you'll be sent to a "Friends & Favorites" page (or you can click through to there by clicking on your name i.e. "Jack's Page" on the top tabs), when you get there you'll see a space to add info on yourself. You can add bio information, your Web site, e-mail and also a picture. I highly recommend you do this as this information will follow any reviews you should make on the Amazon site.

Have People Review Your Book

Very few people buy a "naked" book - meaning that they won't buy a book that has no reviews on it. Have people review your book and add any reviews that you've gotten from other sources!

The Publisher's Page

A page on Amazon will allow you to upload content related to your book to their site. This will allow you to add reviews, descriptive text, bio info and much more. The link for this page is:

http://www.amazon.com/exec/obidos/subst/partners/publishers/publishers.html/102-5354958-1668109

Author Connect

A very cool way to stay in touch with your readers and share exciting and new information is through the new Amazon Author Connect program. All you do is sign up for it, linking all your books, then (using blog technology) you can post whatever you want (relative to your book) through your Author Connect Page. It's a great way to be in front of your readers in a way that's personable and informative. To sign up go to: www.amazon.com/connect.

Amazon.com Reviewers

Take a look at other books similar to yours and see who's reviewed them. If they are Amazon.com reviewers you might want to go after them. Especially if they are one of the top 10 reviewers, these reviewers carry a certain amount of "clout" on the site and with other readers, and many times reviewers like Harriet Klauser (Amazon's #1 reviewer) will send your review out to other sites as well!

Reviewing Books

It's always a good idea to review other books in your genre. When you do this, don't just review from the perspective of a reader, review from the perspective of an expert and make sure to add your contact info (or your Web site) in the review area!

Make a Recommendation!

Recommend an item on Amazon.com similar to yours! This is a great thing to do whenever a new book comes out in your genre.

So You'd Like To... (SYLT) Guides!

This is another great place to promote any articles you've written. You can load your advice/articles/book excerpts onto the So You'd Like To... Guides at Amazon.com by clicking on the "Friends and Favorites" link at the top of the Amazon site, then look for "Write a So You'd Like To..." Guide and start the process. The key here is to make sure you have a list of books you recommend to go with your SYLT guide (including yours!). The links to your article will be featured on each of your recommended book pages.

Using Amazon as an additional promotion tool is a savvy way to make sure your presence on the Net doesn't end with your Web site. Go where the readers go, and in so doing, you'll lead them right to your book.

ONE MINUTE MARKETING

If it weren't for the last minute, nothing would get done.
— Anonymous

So, after all of this are you still not convinced you can market your book? Or maybe you *know* you can market, you just don't know if you can find the time to do so. Well, welcome to the club. Most of the authors I work with or coach work day jobs and try to cram in as much marketing as they can after they come home from an exhausting day at the office. Working this way can be completely overwhelming. It's no wonder most authors only market their books for 90 days. Who could stand to keep up this pace any longer than that? There are so many things authors need to do, most simply don't know where to start.

Enter the one-minute marketer. As tempting as it is, we can't do everything. It's just not realistic. Instead, try doing just three things a day. I found that authors are not only more focused this way but tend to be a hundred times more effective. If you're marketing your own book and you're becoming overwhelmed by the magnitude of the work ahead of you, try doing just three things a day. Some of these will only take you a minute and in one week alone you'll have promoted your book in 15 new ways. And remember, your three things don't have to be earth shattering, they can be as simple as sending a thank you note.

Here are a few ideas you can implement when you've got a minute or two to spare:

- Call your local library and sign up to do a talk. You won't get paid for this, but they will let you sell your book (for a 10% commission back to the library).

- Troll some of the competition's Web sites and see where they are getting their media exposure because those media outlets should be on your target media list too!

- Want to drive more attention to your book? How about creating a contest! Contests are great promotional tools. Design one around the topic of your book. For example, I held a contest asking people for the top 10 things *not* to do when you're marketing your book. Get the idea?

- Still trying to get to know your local media (or trying to get them to notice you?) Why not call up a producer and invite him or her for coffee?

- Pitch your story to a local radio and/or TV station.

- How's your Web site these days? Remember, it's your 24/7 marketing tool so make sure it's up to date.

- And while you're updating your Web site, why not list it on search engines like Google or Alta Vista. Or go over to www.addme.com and let them do it for you…for free!

- Submit an article to a topic-related e-mail newsletter. By now you know that Ezine publishers are always looking for content. If you currently subscribe to an e-mail newsletter that you'd like to contribute to, e-mail the editor and ask what the guidelines are. Or, you can submit your article by registering at the following yahoo group: Publish In Yours (PublishInYours-subscribe@ yahoogroups.com).

- Have you started calling bookstores for signings? Why not start that today?

- Magazine articles are a great way to get exposure. Why not submit an article (or book excerpt) to a topic-related magazine today?

- Are you a member of all the pertinent organizations in your field of writing? If not, you should be. For example, if you wrote a mystery novel you should think about joining a mystery writing group in your area. Not only will you be able to promote your book at meetings, but most groups are always looking for speakers.

Postcard Promo!

How are you staying in touch with your contacts? Are you sending them e-mails on a periodic basis "just to say hi"? Well if you are, you might want to reconsider your connections strategy. Here's why: we live in a world inundated with electronic media. It's nice every once in a while to get a personal note, isn't it? Your postcards should prominently display the cover of your book. When you have your cards in hand get out your top contact list (the folks you want to stay in touch with the most) and start sending out those cards. Whether it's a thank you note or you're just dropping them a line, plan to do your postcard promo every six weeks. Also, if you're out of town doing anything related to your book, remember to bring a stack

of postcards and stamps with you so you can address any thank
you notes right after your meeting or event.

A MARKETING TIMELINE

Strategy and timing are the Himalayas of marketing.
Everything else is the Catskills.
— Al Ries

They say that timing is everything and that's especially true for book promotion. Once your book is available, the clock starts ticking. Now that you're beginning to outline what you're going to do, you'll need to decide when you're going to implement it. Here's a brief outline of what you should plan to do and when:

While book is being printed

√   Create reader profile

√   Begin to pull together a media list

√   Determine your hook or hooks

√   Start highlighting dates on the calendar you will use to promote yourself

√   Put together your press kit

√   Make sure your Web site is up and running and ready to go for your book launch

√   Start gathering a list of special sales possibilities

√   Put together your association list for any potential public
     speaking or special sales opportunities

Four Months Prior to Publication Date

√   Send packets out for signings or speaking events to
     coincide with your release date.

√   Prepare and send packets to prepublication date
     reviewers.

√   Send packets to book clubs.

√   If you're going after the national magazine market, now
     is the time to send out these packets.

√   If you're going after the national TV show market, now
     is the time to send out these packets.

Three Months Prior to Publication Date

√   Send out special sales packets.

√   Send books to catalogs for catalog sales.

√   If you have a topic worthy of major media attention pitch
     it now if you need to have your interview coincide with
     the release date of your book.

√   Start gathering potential media and activities for your
     local promotion.

One Month Prior to Publication Date

√   Go through your list of media contacts, make sure they
     are current – add to them if necessary.

√   Start pitching yourself to radio.

√ Start pitching yourself to the newspaper market.

√ Confirm signings and other events.

Your Book is Available

√ Start pitching radio shows for interviews.

√ Plan to do media announcements around your signings and events.

√ Submit your book to additional post-publication date reviewers.

Ongoing Promotional Activities

√ Keep pitching radio.

√ Pitch holidays and special events appropriate to your topic.

√ Keep pitching yourself to speaking events and signings.

√ Don't forget to send thank you notes as appropriate for your ongoing activities.

√ Keep doing whatever you can as long as it makes sense for your book!

A WORLD OF THANKS

Nothing is more honorable than a grateful heart.
— Seneca

One of the best ways to build relationships is to remember to thank people. I personally send thank you notes all the time. I send them after an interview. I send them to a media person who was considering my story but decided to postpone it for a while: "Thanks for taking the time to consider XYZ." I send one to the bookstore that hosted my signing. I even send it to the people that say "no." Thank them for taking the time to speak with you and thank them for considering your story idea, event or whatever it was you were pitching them. Trust me, they will remember you. Send them a card, not an e-mail. Preferably send them a postcard with your book cover on the front and a handwritten thank you note on the back.

Think about it this way. You buy your neighbor's son a gift for graduation. He doesn't send a thank you note. When he gets married, you get him a gift as well. Again, you're ignored. Now, when that baby shower comes around what do you think you'll be getting them? You got it. It works the same in business. We're so busy and caught up in our lives and our own plans that we often forget to thank those people who are just as busy as we are and still took the time to listen to us.

Remember, you need them more than they need you. So when you're putting together your marketing plan, add "send thank-you notes" to your list. I guarantee you won't be disappointed by the results.

A FEW FINAL WORDS

Never, ever, ever, ever give up.
— *Winston Churchill*

Success comes in all shapes and sizes. For some, it's finally getting national media recognition, for others it's holding their finished book in their hand. But moreover, it's making a difference. When you get discouraged and when nothing seems to be working, remember why you got into this business in the first place. I don't mean to sound like Pollyanna about this, but there were days when all that got me through was a personal commitment I made to myself long ago. I used to say that if I could transport one person for an hour or two out of his or her own life and maybe help him or her in some way or allow that person to forget his or her own worries, then I have achieved my goal. Everyone who realizes they have literary blood coursing through their veins knows the passion that is at times all-consuming.

Whatever you choose to do with the information in this book, know this: you have, right now, the opportunity to change or enhance someone's life. It is a gift that cannot and should not be ignored. It may not be something you do now, but know that the author in you will always try to come out. It is a voice that will never be silenced.

Becoming an author is not really a profession you choose, but rather it chooses you. There are days when I wish I did not have to write. Some days it's more like a curse than anything else. But when we put pen to paper and the words seduce us into writing more, there's nothing else in the world like it.

SECTION NINE

RESOURCE GUIDE

To follow without halt, one aim; there is the secret of success. And success? What is it? I do not find it in the applause of the theater; it lies rather in the satisfaction of accomplishment.
— Anna Pavlova

BOOKS

Deval, Jacqueline. *Publicize Your Book!* Penguin Putnam Pub: 2003

D'Vari, Marisa. *Media Magic; Grow Rich in Your Niche* Business Communication Press Pub: 2004

Ensign, Paulette. *How to Promote Your Business with Booklets* Tips Products International Pub: 2000

Jud, Brian. *Beyond the Bookstore.* Publishers Weekly Pub: 2004

Kremer, John. *1001 Ways to Market Your Book.* Open Horizons Pub: 2006

Poynter, Dan. *The Self Publishing Manual.* ParaPublishing Pub: 2006

Reis, Fern. *The Publishing Game.* Peanut & Jelly Press Pub: 2003

Ross, Marilyn and Tom. *Jump Start Your Book Sales.* Communication Creativity Pub: 1999

Sansevieri, Penny. *No More Rejections. Get Published Today!* Morgan James Publishing. Pub: 2006

HELPFUL WEB SITES

Author Event Promotion

- Publishers Weekly – a great resource to list your author event or book tour. Here's the link for submitting your information: http://publishersweekly.reviewsnews.com/index.asp?layout=authorsMain

- Netread.com – they have a database of upcoming events you can search as well as an area where you can submit your own event to their site. They also offer many articles, helpful links and great information for anyone publishing and promoting their book.

- Writerswrite.com/events – another great place to announce your event, it will appear in their newsletter which goes out to thousands of authors each week.

- Going on the road? Don't forget to list yourself with "Authors on the Highway" at www.bookwire.com/bookwire/NetRead/index.html. This site is viewed by both the general public as well as industry professionals.

- Are you an expert? If you are, try getting a listing at Yearbook (www.yearbook.com). These books get mailed out to the media on a yearly basis. If they're ever in need of an expert and they find your listing in Yearbook, you might just get a call.

Writing & Publishing Organizations

- Publishers Marketing Association – a terrific organization to belong to whether you've published one book or 20. They also have their yearly "Publisher's University" which precedes the BEA (Book Expo America). A not to be missed educational and networking program! (www. pma-online.org)

- Small Publishers Association of North America (SPAN) – helps publishers and authors stay in touch with the industry and keep on top of their individual marketing campaigns. Offering a terrific newsletter and several educational programs, a membership here is always a great idea. (www.spannet.org)

- Small Press Center – a great place for programs and events related to publishing. They always have a number of educational programs to choose from. (www.smallpress. org)

- National Writers Union – the only union representing writers in all genres, formats, and media working in the U.S. market. (www.nwu.org)

- The Authors Guild – offers several benefits including e-mail alerts and bulletins; seminars and a contract service department. They can also help you with rights, e-rights, copyright issues and taxes. Membership requires that you've published at least one book or three articles. (www.authorsguild.org)

- American Society of Journalists and Authors – offers an annual conference, newsletter, writer referral service, professional resource lists, and online discussion forums. (www.asja.org)

- Romance Writers of America – has a variety of benefits including a newsletter, local networking group, an annual conference, professional seminars, contests and awards. (www.rwanational.com)

- Sisters in Crime – has a special focus on women mystery writers and offers a number of benefits to their members including a newsletter, support of special interest groups, minorities, and new writers. (www.sistersincrime.org)

- Mystery Writers of America – offers an annual meeting, national and chapter newsletters, discounts on magazines, books, car rentals, hotels, and insurance, they also offer a mentor program and annual literacy awards. (www. mysterywriters.org)

Online Newsletters & E-mail Newsgroups

- Writing for Dollars – get free tips and tricks for maximizing your marketing dollars. Send an e-mail to Wfd-subscribe@topica.com.

- Get Published - Stay current with news from the publishing industry as well as marketing ideas and tips in this free bi-weekly e-mail newsletter. To subscribe send an e-mail to get-published-subscribe@topica.com

- John Kremer's Book Marketing Tip of the Week – This newsletter really keeps me motivated to market, market, market. For your free subscription, send an e-mail to johnkremer@bookmarket.com.

- Writerswrite.com – subscribe to this newsletter and keep abreast of what events are upcoming in the world of writing.

- Publish-L - One of the most helpful discussion lists I belong to is at www.publish-l.com. Peruse the Web site and read (and adhere to) their guidelines. You won't regret becoming a member of this highly informative group of people. There's a wealth of knowledge here, and I can't tell you how much I've learned from these folks.

- WritersWeekly.com – a great site and offers a weekly newsletter. To subscribe send an e-mail to writemarkets-subscribe@egroups.com

- The Daily Grind – Looking for ways to successfully navigate your life as a writer? This bi-weekly newsletter provides insightful tips and news writers can use. Send an e-mail to CHDailyGrind-subscribe@topica.com.

- Self Publishing - Interested in swapping ideas with other authors in the midst of promoting their books? Send an e-mail to self-publishing-subscribe@yahoogroups.com

- Get Published Today! - Need empowerment? Don't we all. Try sending an e-mail message to get-published-subscribe@yahoogroups.com. This is a group dedicated to inspiring and empowering authors to keep them on track. They also share tips, tricks and media contacts. Great site!

- The Idea Lady – a great newsletter packed with marketing tips, published online every Tuesday. Subscribe to this newsletter by going to Cathy Stucker's site at www.idealady.com or by sending an e-mail to ideasub@idealady.com

- Publisher's Lunch – a wealth of daily information on the publishing industry, new deals, pending deals and of course, a tad of industry gossip thrown in for good measure (www.publisherslunch.com)

- The Book Marketing Expert Newsletter - is a bi-weekly E-zine packed with insider tips on book marketing and promotion. Each issue also comes with our exclusive media leads and magazine profiles. To subscribe send a blank e-mail to mailto: subscribe@amarketingexpert. com

Publicity, Resources & Promotion

- Para Publishing – a site maintained by the King of self-publishing, Dan Poynter. It's filled with publishing info, special reports and a great (ok, awesome) newsletter. (www.parapublishing.com)

- Literary Leaps – a great place to list your book-related Web site. (www.literaryleaps.com)

- Books XYZ – Looking for another outlet to sell and promote your book? Try Books XYZ. A basic listing is free. If you want your cover photo on there it's $25. You do your own shipping for them, but they only require a 15% commission on every sale. (www.booksxyz.com)

- Bookwire.com – really helps keep you on top of what's going on in the industry. They offer a section for promotion, event listings and regular e-mail updates.

- Wordmuseum.com – a great resource to list your book, purchase advertising or submit an author interview.

- Writershelpdesk.com – a very useful Web site for authors, filled with links, reports and helpful advice.

- Association of Booksellers – great site to locate bookstores and media materials. (www.bookweb.org/)

- FreelanceWriters.com - If you're looking for work as a freelancer, check out http://www.freelancewriting.com/. It's a great resource of information for writers looking to gain exposure and it's also a searchable database for people looking to hire freelancers for projects. This is not a free service to the author (it's free if you're doing the hiring), but the sign up fee is minimal.

- Bookgnome – a great place to list your books for free. (www.ignome.com/books/submission/)

- Bookmarket.com – this site by John Kremer is a cornucopia of information to get you started and keep you going.

- Sharpwriter.com – offers tons of great information for writers, including a dictionary (can't have too many of those), a quotation section and an information area on grammar and punctuation.

- Ideasiteforbusiness.com – chock full of great advice, although more general in nature, I always seem to come away with at least a grain of new information. Sometimes that's all it takes.

- Freelancewrite.about.com - a great resource for freelancers with links and helpful tips on writing, publishing, and marketing. Don't miss out on this one.

- Authorsden.com - a great place for authors to show their stuff. Grab yourself a profile page and start telling the world about your book. While you're there, take a look at my page on Author's Den at www.authorsden.com/visit/ author.asp?id=1221

- Schoolbookings.com – a great place to register yourself if you're interested on obtaining speaking engagements at schools. Registration is $99 for one year.

- Tradepub.com – if you're looking for trade publications in your topic or area of expertise, you can browse their list of over 300 publications. Subscriptions to the various trade publications are free to professionals who qualify.

Media, Media, Media

- If you're trying to track down print or broadcast media in a particular genre or city, take a peek at www.newsdirectory. com. They've got over 17,000 listings from all over the world.

- If you're looking for articles relevant to your topic or area of expertise, shoot on over to www.journalistexpress. com.

- Blue Eagle – locating media professionals just became a bit easier. With links to more than 700 newspaper and magazine columnists, Blue Eagle is a terrific resource for any savvy PR pro. (www.blueeagle.com)

- NewsDirectory – your guide to all online English-language media. This is a free directory of newspapers, magazines, TV stations, even colleges, visitors' bureaus and government agencies. (www.newsdirectory.com)

- Mr. Magazine – each month this magazine sleuth gives you the heads up on which magazines are hot and which are not. (www.mrmagazine.com)

- If you're having a tough time locating an article that appeared in a daily newspaper because you don't know the name of the newspaper, then head on over to www. newspaperlinks.com. They have papers listed by state, city, and region. Once in their site you can find your paper and click through to the Web site.

- No budget for a press-clipping service? Well, not to worry. Google has a great news site that will help you keep track of key words and/or when, where and how you are mentioned in the news. Just go to www.news. google.com and click on "News Alerts." You'll need to supply them with the keywords to search for and an e-mail address the search results can be sent to. It's fast, easy, and very thorough!

News Sites

- Remember it's important for any campaign to position yourself on a current news trend. So, what's in the news? Here's where you can find out www.daypop.com/news/ or www.news.google.com

- If you're interested in finding out what the hot topics are that people are searching for, take a look at Ask Jeeves. (http://static.wc.ask.com/docs/about/jeevesiq.html?o=0)

Publishing Info, Trends and Updates

- Publishing Central – helps you stay current on all the publishing news. Here you can learn about industry associations, current news, book trends and statistics on book sales. (www.publishingcentral.com)

- BookWire – offers daily publishing news, literary events, and a wealth of industry links. (www.bookwire.com)

- Trendwatching – a great newsletter that will help you stay on top of trends. The newsletter is free, log onto the site to subscribe. (www.trendwatching.com)

- Trend spotting anyone? If you're looking to stay one step ahead of the future, the following links will help you do just that. Each focuses on forecasting and future trends. Great if you're looking to anchor your book on the latest hot new thing.

  www.wfs.org

  www.iftf.org

  www.burrus.com

  www.herman.net

  www.faithpopcorn.com

Research, Statistical, and Legalese Related Sites:

- Libraryspot.com – great site for research!

- Findarticles.com – a vast archive of published articles you can search for free. I can't tell you how often I've used this site, and it's constantly updated.

- EarlyAmerica.com – the site to visit if you're looking for information relating to life in early America. It's filled with all sorts of links, photos, maps and essays detailing the life our forefathers led.

Don't reinvent the wheel, instead go to www.search-it-all. com/government/forms1/aspx

- to find a terrific resource of legal forms including subcontractor agreements, contracts, and more!

- Yourdictionary.com - an excellent collection of dictionary portals. This site offers links to a huge selection of language dictionaries, including dictionaries for rare (vanishing) languages, a good selection of Native American language dictionaries, plus translation tools and grammar.

- Looking for some statistics straight from the government? Head on over to www.fedstats.com

- Another dictionary that allows you to look up the meaning of a word from a variety of different sources is www.onelook.com. This dictionary will also help locate slang and medical dictionaries.

- Here's a dictionary for the true skeptic. A critical survey of questionable therapies, eccentric beliefs, amusing deceptions, and dangerous delusions. (www.skepdic.com)

- Any research you are doing relative to our 50 states just got easier with www.50states.com. It's a treasure trove of state-by-state information. Each time you click on one state it will take you to a wealth of information helpful to any writer trying to get a background on a particular part of the country.

- Another great site for statistics on just about everything is www.statistics.com.

- Refdesk.com - refers to itself as "The single best source for facts on the Net." There's an incredible list of dictionaries, almanacs, encyclopedias and much, much more.

AFTERWORD
MARKETING SECRETS LEAKED
FROM THE PUBLISHER'S OFFICE

This chapter was graciously contributed by David L. Hancock, the Founder of Morgan James Publishing.

I am grateful to David and Morgan James Publishing for accepting this book for publication. If you know anything about traditional publishers, then you know that they are not usually very easy to work with. Some authors wait months and even years to hear back from a traditional publisher before even getting an audience to talk about their book.

I found Morgan James to be completely different, but with still all of the benefits of working with a traditional, New York publishing house. David shared with me at one point that the largest book wholesaler in the world had nicknamed his company "The Entrepreneurial Publisher". I quite frankly agree.

It is my privilege to be able to share these cutting-edge publishing secrets with you.

Publishing Secrets

When Penny approached me about this book I was very excited. After all, I publish books. With more than 335 titles in

FROM BOOK TO BESTSELLER

print the more my authors can learn about how to promote and market their books, the better it is for Morgan James.

If you have read this book all the way through and not just skipped to the back section here, you have more information that you could probably ever implement on how to make your book wildly success and even turn it into a bestseller.

Penny asked me to explain to you a few tips that you could use to make sure you profit as much as possible from the success of your book. My background is in marketing. Before I became a publisher, I was a home builder, mortgage banker and Guerrilla Marketing coach.

From all of the marketing training I've taken (as well as what I've gleaned from my authors over the years) I've found there are some very specific things you can do with your book to make it a powerful business building tool, as well as an income generator.

As a publisher, I can tell you honestly, that the bulk of the money authors can make does not come just from the royalties of their book. The real money is made when you stop to consider what you book can do for you. Penny has addressed many of the key points and I have a couple of additional suggestions that may be of good value to you.

When writing your book, make sure you do the following things to maximize your earnings:

1. Build your marketing list. One of the most powerful lessons I learned from my marketing authors is that you don't make most of your money the first time a customer buys something from you. You make the majority of your income when that person, who lets say bought your book, becomes a life-long customer and continues to spend money with you. It

doesn't matter whether you have other books, are a coach or consultant, or have educational tools or programs—your real income will come from those higher dollar purchases down the road.

To build your marketing list, you need a way of finding out who bought your book. One of the common misunderstandings new authors have is that they think they will know who buys their book in the bookstore. It doesn't happen that way. But the way that you can find out who purchased your book is to create a compelling bonus offer in the book that has them go online and supply their name and email to get that bonus offer.

2.   Next, you need to find some way of giving the reader extra benefit when they get to the end of your book. Many authors make the mistake of simply writing a book and then after they deliver a ton of wonderful content, simple end the book by saying "The End". In my opinion, that is disappointing to me. When I read books, and I like the material, I wind up falling in love with the author and wanting to have more. You can give your readers more by simply producing a product, like an audio recording of the book, and making it available at the end of the book. Promise me, your readers will thank you.

Because of the close relationship that Morgan James has with Penny, she asked me if I would be willing to do something exceptional for her readers. She asked if we would be willing to open up our doors to review manuscripts or book ideas from her readers. While we receive about 3,000 submissions a year, it sounded like a good idea to me, so I said... yes.

So as a favor to Penny, if you have a book idea or manuscript that you would like reviewed by a major New York publisher, take this book to your computer, turn it on, and go to www.Morgan-James.com/booktobestseller. Complete the form and we will be in touch with you to review your book idea or manuscript. To your success!

— David L. Hancock

Founder, Morgan James Publishing

NEED A SPEAKER?

Penny would love to speak at your upcoming event!

Please contact her office at:

(858) 560-0121

or e-mail her at speaker@amarketingexpert.com for more information!

Here is a list of some of her speaking topics:

- Get Published in Ninety Days or Less!
- Stay out of the Rejection Pile!
- Finish Writing Your Book...Now!
- Build Your Business with Books; Get Published in 90 Days!
- Super Savvy Self Promotion
- Creating a Book Hook!
- Author Focus
- Striking Internet Gold
- Networking Gold
- Thinking Outside the Bookstore Box
- Contests: The Good, The Bad and the Ugly
- Media Training Magic
- Getting on Radio and TV Today
- Book Signing Gold

INDEX

SPECIAL OFFER!

$400 worth of red hot marketing tools, a special gift for Book to Bestseller readers!

Here's what you'll get:

- Our powerful audio CD packed with marketing tips and advice, everything you need to sell your book – now!

- Twelve issues of the Book Marketing Expert Newsletter. This newsletter has been called the best in the business, filled with media leads and marketing wisdom there's a wealth of information in each edition.

- Our exclusive Top 50 Media Contacts including producer names at Oprah, Good Morning America and The Today Show!

Ready to get your free gifts?

Come visit us at:

www.booktobestseller.com

to grab yours today!

Printed in the United States
65087LVS00003B/85-300

9 781600 370854